REIGN DOWN

CHANGE YOUR LIFE THROUGH
THE GIFT OF REPENTANCE

REIGN DOWN

WALT KALLESTAD
SHAWN-MARIE COLE

HOWARD BOOKS
A DIVISION OF SIMON & SCHUSTER
New York   London   Toronto   Sydney

Our purpose at Howard Books is to:
- *Increase faith* in the hearts of growing Christians
- *Inspire holiness* in the lives of believers
- *Instill hope* in the hearts of struggling people everywhere

Because He's coming again!

Published by Howard Books, a division of Simon & Schuster, Inc.
1230 Avenue of the Americas, New York, NY 10020
www.howardpublishing.com

Reign Down © 2008 Walt Kallestad and Shawn-Marie Cole

Library of Congress Cataloging-in-Publication Data

Reign down : change your life through the gift of repentance / Walt Kallestad and Shawn-Marie Cole.
    p.   cm.   2007038949

ISBN-13: 978-1-4165-6271-9
ISBN-10:   1-4165-6271-0

10 9 8 7 6 5 4 3 2 1

For information regarding special discounts for bulk purchases, please contact: Simon & Schuster Special Sales at 1-800-456-6798 or business@simonandschuster.com.

Edited by Mary McNeil
Design by Davina Mock-Maniscalco

Above all we humbly and gratefully dedicate this book to our Lord and Savior, Jesus Christ, whose life mission—"repent and believe"—has become our life passion. We are also very thankful for our family, which never gets weary of supporting us to pursue God's own heart. We love you, Brian; Sevannah and Ashlin and Mary; Patrick and Shannon.

Think you the bargain's hard, to have exchanged
The transient for the eternal, to have sold
Earth to buy heaven?

Paulinus of Nola

CONTENTS

CONTENTS

FOREWORD

I have known Walt Kallestad for years, as we have served on a variety of projects together. Walt is the kind of person you always want on your team. He is a "get it done" kind of guy, and whenever he takes on a project, you can know he does it with prayer and enthusiasm. I am so thankful that he is my friend.

Here is what I like about this new book from Walt & Shawn-Marie: First of all, it begins with the understanding of the need to allow God to reign in one's life. It acknowledges that when a person has faith (trust) in God, he makes the choice to submit his own will to the will of God. This is a critical step in receiving the blessings that God has in store for believers. Learning about how to let God reign in your life is liberating. It does not restrict your choices, but rather it empowers the believer to live an exciting life.

Secondly, I like the personal transformation that this book speaks to. We all know that sometimes pain and failure in one's past shackle so many. In this book the authors talk about how a believer can move beyond those pains and failures. Each chapter gives biblical teaching on the subject of how vital repentance is to this whole process of transformation. Everyone has areas in his or her life that need to be transformed. This book will help the reader make those transformations.

Thirdly, I love the hope that this book offers the reader. Its pages are full of stories of hope and blessing. They illustrate how, every day, people have faced the same type of hurts as the reader, and yet have learned how to move beyond those hurts. This is the kind of book that God can use in a powerful way to change lives. Let this message have a dynamic impact in your life.

—Dr. Robert H. Schuller,
founding pastor of the
Crystal Cathedral

REIGN
DOWN

PROLOGUE

A hot desert breeze blew against Nahum's face, stinging his dry, parched skin. He'd spent all day standing in the sun atop the rock. The rock. Marwa-Jonah, a quartz outcropping on a hill east of the city that marked the place where Bedouin tradition said Jonah had stood and watched with sadness as Nineveh blossomed and grew. That was a long time ago.

Nahum took a deep breath.

Oh, that it was so this day.

Behind Nahum the Zagros Mountains towered, the jagged peaks already softening in the purple glow of the afternoon light. In front of him a great plain stretched flat and smooth as far as the eye could see, broken only by the thin ribbon of the Tigris River and the outline of the buildings of Nineveh. As Nahum watched, the buildings seemed to dance in the shimmering waves of heat that rose from the sand.

Even from that distance he heard the clank of steel as the armies of the Medes and Babylonians wreaked havoc on the city. He could not help but imagine the horror of that fight as men hacked and sliced each other to death. By now, the living would be standing on the flesh of the dead. Their blood would have turned the streets to mud. The men of Nineveh who remained would have long since lost hope of saving the city. At this late hour they would be fighting only to protect their own lives. The images in his mind sent a shudder through Nahum's body.

As the afternoon wore on, the desert breeze grew stronger. Grains of sand pelted his arms and legs. His eyes narrowed as the sand struck his cheeks. Through the thin slits of his eyelids he saw a column of smoke rise from a building to the left. A moment later, the smoke turned black and heavy. Before long, smoke rose from a building to the right. Soon, all but the dome of the palace disappeared as a wall of fire moved across the city.

Nahum watched and remembered the day he first realized destruction would come. Almost three years ago, it seemed like only yesterday. He'd been out for a walk a little before dusk and had just come in for the evening. After a drink from the water jar by the door, he moved his mat to a spot beneath the window and lay down to rest. It was the first cool evening of the year. He was almost asleep when an image in his mind jarred him awake. That image was quickly followed by another. Then another. Each more awful than the one before. When the last one disappeared from his mind, he heard the words of the great oracle. The Oracle of the Almighty. An oracle that spelled the end of Nineveh.

The LORD is slow to anger and great in power;
the LORD will not leave the guilty unpunished.
His way is in the whirlwind and the storm,

PROLOGUE

And clouds are the dust of
his feet. (Nahum 1:3)

Nineveh. A city of splendor and beauty. Three days across in every direction. The largest city anyone had ever seen. You could find all the latest there. Beautiful fabric from Ur. Pots from the cities beyond the mountains near the sea. Spices from the lands beyond the desert to the east. Canals brought fresh water from the mountains, and there was everything imaginable to eat.

Still, for all the city had to offer, Nineveh had forgotten the words that had come to it long ago. The men of Nineveh had let them fade from their lips. The words had vanished from their songs. They'd forgotten the message they'd received from Jonah son of Amittai. Those had been words of mercy. Words of grace. Words they had received and believed. Words that had changed the city, at least for a time. Now, those words were nowhere to be found. Erased from the halls of the city's buildings. Stricken from its columns and monuments. And gone from the Ninevites' minds, too. Oblivious, they'd eaten and danced and slept as the time of grace slipped past. Now there was only judgment.

Nahum ran his hand across his cheek. He shifted his weight to the opposite foot and gave a long, sorrowful sigh.

In the west, the sun sank toward the horizon. Soon, it would slip out of sight on the far side of the plain. The desert breeze was now a strong wind. Sand swirled around Nahum in a cloud. Nineveh disappeared from sight, but as the wind rushed past, it brought the sound of men crying out in agony. The smell of burning buildings and the stench of smoldering flesh stung his nostrils.

Nahum gathered his cloak around his shoulders and covered his head. In the darkness of that moment, one thought kept repeating.

It didn't have to be this way.

CHAPTER 1

REIGN DOWN

Let it rain, let it rain.

Open the floodgates of heaven.

—MICHAEL W. SMITH, "LET IT RAIN"

Tears welled in her eyes as she stared out at the faces of her classmates. With trembling hands she gripped both sides of the podium and held on, hoping she wouldn't turn and run. Below, out of sight behind the podium, her knees shook from side to side. Muscles in her legs ached. She struggled to find the courage to speak.

All the while, her thoughts raced in a thousand directions.

Will they laugh at me? Will they pay attention? No one will believe me. No one will ever speak to me again. I'm so weird. I can't do this. I have to do this.

She took a breath and from somewhere inside her, words began to slip from between her lips.

"You don't know me." Her voice quivered. She kept going. "You know my name. You know my face. But you don't know me."

She paused and took another breath. Her knees still shook

but her hands no longer trembled. Still, her heart pounded in her chest as she came to what she must say next.

"When I was in the sixth grade, two boys . . . two boys raped me."

The room was suddenly quiet. Students who'd been fidgeting and squirming in their seats became still and motionless. All eyes were fixed on her.

Their reaction gave her confidence. Her voice grew steadier as she continued.

"They took me out behind the gym at the school where I used to go and . . . that's where it happened. That's where they did it. I wanted to tell someone, but I was ashamed and mad and wondering what I'd done to make them do that to me. I thought maybe there was something wrong with me, so I kept quiet."

As the audience listened, she told how the emotional pain of that sexual violation led her into a life of promiscuity. She moved from one relationship to another trying to find the acceptance, the sense of self that had been violated that afternoon by those boys in those awful minutes behind the gym.

When relationships failed to fill the void in her life, she began hanging out with friends who had access to alcohol. She told about sneaking alcohol from her parents, from the parents of friends, and about getting it from older friends who obtained it for her. She drank to be accepted by her friends, and she drank until her emotions were numb, drowning the pain and humiliation she wanted so much to hide. Many mornings she arrived at school already drunk. At home she was rebellious, ill-tempered. Her relationship with her parents was difficult, at best.

Then, on a mission trip with a group from church, she came

in contact with people even more desperate than she. People who faced poverty and misery in a way she'd never seen before, but who were being transformed by the Holy Spirit in spite of their circumstances. As she worked with the group from church, the Holy Spirit began to speak to her about how He could transform her, too.

On the bus ride home from that mission trip, she found herself face-to-face with the Holy Spirit and face-to-face with the life she'd been living. Tears began to stream down her face. A friend saw what was happening and moved to the seat beside her. Soon a group gathered around her. They listened as she told her story. When she finished, they began to pray with her and for her. There in the back of the bus she got on her knees and repented of all she'd done. She repented and turned to Jesus.

Telling her story on the bus that day, she'd found release from the pain of the past. Now, telling it there in the auditorium to her teachers and classmates, she found not only freedom from the past but also healing for it. The fear that had kept her searching, the lies that had led her to a life of rebellion, fell away.

She paused a moment and scanned the room, letting her eyes make contact with faces of people she knew, many of them her friends. Confidence now replaced the fear she'd felt when she began. Her knees no longer shook. The ache in her legs was gone. She knew what to say next, and she said it with authority.

"I found the love I was looking for when I repented and turned my life over to Jesus. Some of you here today need to do that. You need to repent. You need to turn your life over to Jesus and let Him have control. And I invite you to do that right now."

When she finished, she backed away from the podium and

took a seat. For the longest time, no one moved. Then, one by one, students rose from their seats and came to the front. There, they knelt and prayed, crying out to God, turning to Him, some of them for the first time.

That one-hour service lasted another two hours. When students were dismissed, the movement of the Holy Spirit that began in the auditorium continued into the classrooms. Students and teachers alike found themselves transformed in a revival that swept through the entire school. Home groups formed for discipleship through Bible study, prayer, and mutual support. The entire school was transformed. So was the church.

That transformation was made possible because one fourteen-year-old girl turned to God in repentance, then shared her experience with those around her. Through one girl, one act of repentance, one life, God was able to reach a school, a church, a community. Through that one event, God gained access to many lives, lives once ruled by self, by idols, by many of the other gods they'd made for themselves. Through that one act, He was able to establish His rule, His reign, His kingdom in their lives, and He was able to rain down His mercy and grace in a transforming movement of the Holy Spirit that continues to this day.

The same power that transformed that girl and that school can transform our nation. Not through some act of "national repentance" but through individual acts of repentance as we each turn to God in humility, as we each lay aside all the other things we've worshiped and let Him reign in our lives. Let Him Reign Down in us and through us—ruling our lives and pouring out His presence upon us.

To you have been given the keys to the kingdom.
Slip the key of repentance into the lock on your heart, and
God will open the door to the rest of your life. Let Him reign in your life,
and He will rain down His mercy, His grace.
He will pour out upon you the gift of His presence in your life.

CHAPTER 2
THE KEY

I will place on his shoulder the key to the house of David;

what he opens no one can shut,

and what he shuts no one can open.

—ISAIAH THE PROPHET, SON OF AMOZ, ISAIAH 22:22

R epent.

Thousands of pages have been written about repentance. Scholars have parsed it down to the last syllable. They have divided it into categories—true repentance, false repentance—and into types: repentance of the heart, repentance of the mind. Still, it's just one simple word.

Repent.

In English it's a word with six letters. The most common Greek word for it is a little longer: *metanoia*.[1] Eight letters, still not very long. But in the first three gospels, that eight-letter word is presented as the key that unlocks the kingdom of God. Fit that key into the lock on your heart, and you can enter the most powerful kingdom of all eternity.

If you're like most of us, the word *repent* brings to mind all kinds of negative images. A scowling preacher dressed in black, shouting from behind a pulpit, hand in the air, sweat dripping from his brow, the congregation cowering before him in the pews. His voice is angry and loud. His words are punctuated by a finger that wags up and down as his hand rises above his head, then slices through the air and stops at an angle that seems to leave it pointing straight toward you. Like a knife, it cuts you to the core, exposing all the ugly, vile secrets of your life. What his finger doesn't reach, his eyes lay bare as they pierce the thin veil of decency behind which you've been hiding. Guilt stabs you in the chest. All the while you wish you were somewhere else.

Trailing close behind that image is a long list. You know the one I'm talking about. The dreaded list of don'ts: Don't drink; don't smoke; don't hang around with those who do—a list that only gets longer and heavier each time you fail to live up to its expectations. Much of my own life has been spent under a merciless hammer of guilt generated by a lengthy list of impossible and irrelevant don'ts.

Yet when you look at Scripture, you can't avoid the call to repentance at the heart of Jesus's message. It's there right from the beginning.

"'The time has come,' He said. 'The kingdom of God is near. Repent and believe the good news'" (Mark 1:15).

Good news?

Those glaring eyes behind that accusing finger pointed at my face are bringing me good news?

Could it be that the image we have of repentance isn't what Jesus had in mind? What if all our preconceived notions about repentance are wrong? Suppose, instead of being heavy-handed, guilt-laden condemnation, the call to repentance is an invitation?

An invitation to freedom. An invitation to join a truly magnificent kingdom. An invitation to an incredible adventure of unbelievable proportion. A gift.

Would you ignore it because the thought of it made you . . . uncomfortable?

Think about it like this: Suppose for a moment that you haven't been feeling well. You stumble around the house for a week, hacking and coughing. Finally, your spouse or a family member or friend shoves you into the car and takes you to the doctor. He looks you over, listens to your lungs, and makes a few x-ray images of your chest. After a while he comes back to the examination room, glances over your chart, and gives you a grim look.

"You have pneumonia."

You nod. "I guess that's why I can't raise my arm to brush my teeth without stopping to rest."

He smiles a knowing smile. "That would be it." The look on his face turns serious. "Fluid has filled the bottom portion of your right lung."

A frown wrinkles your brow. "Fluid?"

He nods again. "Mucus."

You still have a blank look.

He tries again. "The green stuff you cough into a handkerchief."

Your stomach turns. Yes, you've seen it. You've tasted it. Even now, your body shudders at the thought. The doctor smiles again and shrugs.

"Don't worry." He takes a prescription pad from the pocket of his jacket and drops it on his lap. "We can fix it."

From his other pocket he takes a pen and scribbles something on the pad.

At that moment, you have several options. You can dwell on the slimy, nasty, green mucus sloshing in your lung and throw up. You can refuse to think about it, leave the office, and limp home. Or you can take the medicine the doctor is about to give you. Take it, and you'll get well. Take it, and once again you can play outside with your children, go to the beach, laugh and giggle with your spouse, see another sunset. Refuse it, and you will die.

The doctor offers you life. Why would you refuse his remedy just because the thought of your illness makes you . . . sick?

Sound silly?

Jesus used this very same example. You remember the story. He went over to Levi's house for dinner. Levi was a tax collector. People living back then didn't like tax collectors any more than we do today. Someone saw Jesus sitting on the deck out back over at Levi's house, someone with his own "don't" list: Don't cheat; don't steal; and definitely don't hang around with those who do. Jesus was violating that list.

By the time dinner was over, everyone on the block knew Jesus was there. They knew where He was, and they didn't like it. When Jesus came out to go home, some of those neighbors cornered Him between the fence and a tree at the sidewalk. "What do you mean, hanging with Levi? He's a tax collector. A thief."

"You should have eaten with Bill or Jack or Harry. They're good guys. Respectable guys."

"Yeah. Why didn't you call *me*? I'd have fed you."

Jesus offered a simple response, one that cut to the core of both Levi and the neighbors: "It is not the healthy who need a doctor, but the sick."

"Sick? Something wrong?"

"Who's sick? I don't want to catch anything."

"He's not talking about us. Are you, Jesus? There's nothing wrong with us. I mean, after all, we're decent people. We pay our taxes, even if Levi is robbing us. We still pay. We go to synagogue every week. We don't get drunk."

"Well, there was that one time."

"Oh, yeah. You remember that. He was so drunk we had to—"

"All right. All right. He don't need to hear all that. But look, what did He mean by that? 'Only the sick need a doctor'?"

They had their lists, and they did their best to live by them, but the tension of never quite living up to their measure left them feeling angry and bitter. They took out that anger on Jesus, just as we do—on Jesus, on ourselves, and on those around us.

Now, don't misunderstand me. Something is wrong with us. Very wrong. There is something so wrong with us that no list could ever solve it, no matter how closely we followed those interminable don'ts. Something is wrong, and that wrongness has power. It can take away your house, your family, everything you hold dear, even your very life. Making a list only defines the problem. Trying to live up to the list only shows us how far away we are from the solution. It doesn't solve the problem we face.

The problem we face is the lock and chain around our hearts.

Since the beginning of time, we've been told two lies. The first lie is this: God doesn't love you enough to give you His best. He won't take care of you. If He really loved you, you'd have everything this world has to offer. You'd have it all.

That is the lie Eve heard in the garden. It's the lie she told Adam. It's the lie they both believed.

" 'You will not surely die,' the serpent said to the woman. 'For God knows that when you eat of it your eyes will be opened, and you will be like God, knowing good and evil' " (Genesis 3:4–5).

When we believe the first lie, chains wrap around our heart. That's when we're told the second lie: You've messed up now. There's no way out. Your situation is ruined.

Satan tells you a lie and convinces you it's the truth. Then, when you realize you've been had, you've given up the truth in exchange for a lie, he tells you that because you believed a lie, you're ruined.

When you believe that second lie, the lock at the end of those chains around your heart snaps shut.

Don't worry. Jesus has the key. In fact, He has lots of keys—the keys to death, hell, and the grave. And the keys to the kingdom.

There's a key in His hand for the lock on your heart. That key is repentance. It isn't condemnation. It isn't a sentence of judgment or a sentence of death. It isn't a load of guilt or shame. The key of repentance is an invitation. A gift. A doorway that leads to the life you've always wanted to live—a life that, until now, you've never been able to achieve.

That life is made possible when you allow God to reign, when you turn to Him and let Him rule in your heart.

Repent and believe. It's that simple.

I may not be perfect, but my life will never be the same.
I serve a new King.

My tailor friend helped me to understand what I had to do to become a genuine Christian. The key word was do. Those of us standing up front had to decide to do something about what we knew before it could take effect.

He prayed for me and guided me to pray. I had heard the message, and I had felt the inner compulsion to go forward. Now came the moment to commit myself to Christ.

Intellectually, I accepted Christ to the extent that I acknowledged what I knew about Him to be true. That was mental assent. Emotionally, I felt that I wanted to love Him in return for His loving me. But the final issue was whether I would turn myself over to His rule in my life. . . .

No bells went off inside me. No signs flashed across the tabernacle ceiling. No physical palpitations made me tremble. I wondered again if I was a hypocrite, not to be weeping or something. I simply felt a peace. Quiet, not delirious. Happy and peaceful.

—BILLY GRAHAM, *JUST AS I AM*

CHAPTER 3

JUST SAY YES

Jesus did not die to make bad people do good things.
He died to make dead people live.

—LEONARD RAVENHILL

Repentance from better to worse is a change impossible
for us; but it is a noble thing to change from
that which is evil to righteousness.

—*THE MARTYRDOM OF POLYCARP*

R epentance is not a choice between good and bad.
If I had a nickel for every time an adult asked me as a child, "Have you been a good little girl?" I would have enough money to do anything I wanted. All through my childhood, people asked that question. I suppose they wanted to know if I was behaving, but that's not the question they asked. If I could answer that question today, I'd say, "I'm always good. I just don't always act right."

Much of what we're taught about religion today tells us we must strive to be good. That's not just a message you get from religion, either. Much of what we're taught in school and through popular media tells us the same thing. America's cultural religion, that general belief we have in the ability of man to better himself, tells us that same message. The aim of American society is to make life better today than it was yesterday.

The gospel message is not about how good you are. Ask that question of the gospel, and the gospel will reply, "You're never going to be 'good enough.' But you can be redeemed." The question posed by an invitation to the repentance that leads to conversion is not "How good do you want to be?" The question posed by the gospel, the question Jesus is asking you today, is "How alive do you want to be?"

Billy Graham wasn't a bad kid. In fact, it's difficult for me to imagine him doing anything wrong, but I've only known him since he became Billy Graham the evangelist. I didn't know him before then, when he was Billy Frank Graham from Charlotte, North Carolina. Back then, he was just a good kid. He worked on the family farm, went to church on Sunday, did what his parents told him to do—most of the time. If Billy Frank the young teenager walked into your home right now, arm-in-arm with your daughter, you wouldn't hesitate to let him take her out on a date, in your car, with him driving. He was that kind of kid. A good kid.

There was only one problem.

The kingdom of God isn't about how good you are. It's about who you serve. Billy Frank wasn't part of the kingdom of God. He wasn't serving Jesus. He was serving Billy Frank, which put him as far outside the kingdom as any other unrepentant person. Worse, he was trapped in another kingdom. Even at his best, he was a prisoner in the kingdom of Billy Frank.

Until Someone slipped him the key. The key of repentance.

Repentance, the kind that leads to conversion, comes to you in a simple way. You are serving one lord, believing what you think is the truth. Then the Holy Spirit conspires with circumstances, or a word or message, to open your eyes to the truth that there is another way, a way that leads to an unimaginable life of fullness and wholeness. A message that lets you know, deep inside in a place that always suspected the truth, that Jesus is Lord of the universe and that it is your duty to serve Him. The message might come in a church service. It might come from a preacher on television. Perhaps it comes from the echoes of voices that still speak to you from long ago through the Scriptures. Somehow, someway, the Holy Spirit finds you and convinces you.

In response, you stop serving whatever lord you were serving and start serving Jesus. That's the kind of repentance that moves you from the kingdom of darkness to the kingdom of light.

You remember how in Genesis, God came down in the cool of the evening and went for a walk with Adam. They talked about everything. Names for the trees. Names for the animals. The glory of a sunset. The refreshing mist that rose as darkness fell. Whatever they saw, they talked about it. Sometimes they talked about what was on Adam's mind. Other times they talked about what was on God's. Nothing inhibited that conversation. God was right there with Adam. Adam was right there with God.

Everything changed when Adam and Eve listened to the serpent and did what it suggested. You might call it an example of repentance in reverse. They stopped believing the truth and started believing a lie. One bite of the fruit of the forbidden tree, and those quiet walks in the evening became a lot less peaceful. Adam showed up less and had a harder time listening, then he hardly showed up at all.

That's still the way it is today. God wants to come down for a walk with us, only we aren't there. Like Adam, we've been told lies, and we've believed them. Not only that, we've built monuments to those lies, and we've spent all our time tending to those monuments: how we look, how we feel, what the neighbors think, how much money we have, what our credit rating is, where we vacationed last summer, where we're going this year. God wants to go for a walk, but we aren't there.

So, He comes looking for us.

No doubt, God had been after Billy Graham's attention for some time. He finally captured that attention in one of those services with the preacher and the pulpit and the accusing finger I was telling you about earlier. That preacher was a man named Mordecai Ham, an evangelist of legendary zeal for the Lord.

The service Billy Frank attended was held in a large building on the outskirts of Charlotte. Like many others who attended those meetings, he found Jesus when he got out of his seat and went down front at the end of the sermon. He found Jesus, but he didn't find the emotion he saw in others. While some around him responded with tears and cried out in agony, Billy found nothing about the moment emotionally remarkable. Things hadn't turned out as he'd expected, which left him wondering if he'd "gotten it right." Fortunately, he had a friend who helped him.

Repentance isn't complicated. It begins when we respond

with a simple yes to Jesus. In fact, that's all we have to offer. We cannot bring about our own salvation. We cannot earn God's forgiveness. But Scripture makes it plain: There is something we must "do." We must respond. We must "turn." That response, that turning, is simply to say yes.

"Yes, I hear You calling."

"Yes, I know I am far from You."

"Yes, I want to know You."

"Yes" is all we have.

That yes might come from pain deep in your soul. It might be an agonizing plea for help. You might find an act of repentance an emotionally traumatic moment. Many times, the thing that dominates our lives, the lord that controls us and keeps us deceived, has an emotional, embarrassing stigma attached to it. But the focus of repentance isn't on generating an emotion. And it's not about saying the "right" words. It's about turning and changing. Turning from the idols and lords you've previously served—even the idol you may have made of yourself—to the Lord of the universe. Rejecting devotion to one lord and replacing it with devotion to Jesus. That turning begins with the simple response of "Yes, Lord."

You may not have the power within you to change the conduct with which you are confronted. That's fine. The repentance of conversion is not about making you complete all at once. It's about making the turn to Jesus complete. That's all.

Bob Nelson lives in Kentucky. He began his professional life as a golfer. Later, he came to know the Lord and was radically transformed by the experience—a transformation that took him to seminary and to the ordained ministry. One day an acquaintance began asking him questions about Jesus and about Christianity. The conversation went on awhile, and Bob finally asked the man if he was a Christian.

"No, I'm not," the man replied. "I don't think I can become a Christian. I smoke, and if I became a Christian, I'd have to quit smoking, and I can't quit."

When I first heard this, I wondered how many people wish with all their hearts that smoking was the only problem they had. But for that man, smoking was something that dominated his life.

Bob gave him an interesting response. "I tell you what. Jesus isn't worried about your smoking right now. Just come to Him. Just worship Him. You can smoke as long as He lets you."

God's first and primary concern is your salvation, your allegiance to Him. He is first concerned with moving you from the kingdom of darkness to the kingdom of light.

When Walt, my father and coauthor of this book, was called to pastor Community Church of Joy in Arizona, he met a man named Tony Nicoli. Tony had a reputation for being a tough-minded businessman. Most people in Phoenix knew who he was and did their best to stay on his good side. One day he asked Walt about what it took to become a Christian. Instead of giving him a quick answer, Walt said, "Let's go to lunch."

At lunch, he brought the conversation back to the topic.

"So, you want to become a Christian?"

Tony replied, "Oh, I could never do that."

"Why not?"

"I have a really bad past."

Walt tried to assure him that didn't matter.

"Jesus came for everyone—murderers, robbers, prostitutes."

Tony shook his head.

"God could never accept me. My past has been really bad."

For the next few minutes, Walt explained that there wasn't anything for which Jesus didn't offer forgiveness. Slowly, Tony began to soften. After a while he mustered the courage to ask one more question.

"Do you think He could accept me?"

They prayed right there, and with tears streaming down his cheeks, Tony turned his life over to Jesus.

Remember, you are taking a walk with the Holy Spirit. It is hoped that, in this life, it will be a very long walk. That's what He wants. Like the days in the garden with Adam, the Holy Spirit wants to go for a walk with you. That walk is a journey of repentance in which you and He travel deeper and deeper into you, and deeper and deeper into Him. With the repentance of conversion, you are taking the first step.

So, it doesn't matter how repentance feels. It might feel bad. It might feel good. Throwing off a great weight of guilt is liberating. Exposing an ugly area of your life, one you've worked hard to keep hidden, one you've covered with smiles and all the right words—repentance like that might be quite painful. Either way, the emotion you feel isn't the point. Turning and changing your allegiance is.

Repentance is a gift, an invitation. You can accept that gift with the simple response of yes to God. That one response opens the door to your heart, and it opens your heart to His rule and reign. Let Him reign in your heart. Let Him fill you with the gift of His presence.

I put my cigarette out and got down on my knees beside my bed. I'm not sure what I prayed, but I know that I poured my heart out to God and confessed my sin. I told Him I was sorry and that if He would take the pieces of my life and somehow put them back together, I was His. I wanted to live my life for Him from that day forward. I asked Him to forgive me and cleanse me, and I invited Him by faith to come into my life.

That night I had finally decided I was sick and tired of being sick and tired. My years of running and rebellion had ended.

I got off my knees and went to bed.

It was finished.

The rebel had found the cause.

—FRANKLIN GRAHAM,
REBEL WITH A CAUSE

CHAPTER 4

STOP HIDING

Laying down your arms, surrendering, saying you are
sorry, realising that you have been on the wrong track
and getting ready to start life over again from the ground
floor—that is the only way out of a "hole."

—C. S. LEWIS, *MERE CHRISTIANITY*

It's your repentance that counts. Not someone else's.

A few years ago a movie came out called *Sky High.* It's a story about a kid named Will Stronghold. Will is unique in that, unlike the rest of us, his parents are superheroes—Commander and Jetstream—very famous superheroes. When Will is old enough to attend high school, his parents send him to Sky High, a special school created to train the offspring of superheroes. Will arrives there to find everyone expects him to be the next Commander. His father's reputation gives him instant popularity, but that only takes him so far. At Sky High, he has to find his superpower on his own.

Life has a way of bringing us all around to that point. You may have grown up with famous parents. Or maybe you grew up in a small town where your parents were well known and re spected. Those connections can open doors for you, doors that open more easily for you than they do for others. Even so, we all arrive at the same place—the place where we have to stand on our own. Connections can get you the interview, perhaps even get you the job. Whether you keep that job depends on what you do with it. Somewhere along the way, life forces us to move forward on our own.

Not everyone can handle that. Those who can't handle it hide.

Franklin Graham portrays himself as a rebel. I'm sure he thinks of himself that way. When I think of him, I see not so much a rebel but someone who was hiding. He had a nice place to hide. If you were going to hide from God, hiding behind Billy Graham would be a good place. You could easily convince yourself God would never destroy Billy to get to you. That's what Franklin did. He hid behind Billy. He went on mission trips, participated in the work of his father's organization. But his heart was somewhere else. His allegiance was to another.

Franklin thought he was keeping all of that a secret. He did a good job of convincing himself but not many others. Imagine how he felt when his father confronted him. Think about it. Going for a walk with Billy Graham and hearing him say, "You've got to make a choice about whether you're going to serve Jesus." My eyes fill up at the image in my mind of Billy's kind eyes looking into mine, piercing to the depths of my soul.

Franklin could hide behind Billy until Billy moved out of the way. That's what he did. He moved out of the way and let the Holy Spirit confront Franklin on His own terms.

When the Holy Spirit comes looking for us, we all have a tendency to hide. Adam hid behind the largest fig leaves he could find.

> *Then the man and his wife heard the sound of the LORD God as he was walking in the garden in the cool of the day, and they hid from the LORD God among the trees of the garden. But the LORD God called to the man, "Where are you?"*
>
> *He answered, "I heard you in the garden, and I was afraid because I was naked; so I hid."*
>
> *And he said, "Who told you that you were naked?" (Genesis 3:8–11)*

We all have our own hiding places.

Some of us hide behind family. Your father might not have been a famous evangelist. Maybe he was a lawyer or a judge. Perhaps your mother was a respected teacher. My own father pastors a large church. I hid behind him for a long time. Some of us hide behind our standing in the community, what we've achieved in our professions, what we've accomplished in business or sports.

Hiding is the worst option. David wrote in the Psalms,

> *When I kept silent,*
> *my bones wasted away*
> *through my groaning all day long.*
> *For day and night*
> *your hand was heavy upon me;*
> *my strength was sapped*
> *as in the heat of summer.*

Then I acknowledged my sin to you
and did not cover up my iniquity.
I said, "I will confess
my transgressions to the LORD"—
and you forgave
the guilt of my sin. (Psalm 32:3–5)

What makes hiding so bad is that we're hiding from the only One who can rescue us. God is the only One who can put our marriages back together. The only One who can fill the emptiness, the loneliness, the despair. The only One who can unravel all those things that have us entangled—the addiction, the habit, the destruction. He is the only One who can unlock the chains of deception that keep our hearts in bondage. Only He can give us a future, a destiny. And not just any destiny but a hope that resonates with the deepest longings of our hearts—not the desires we can articulate but the desires buried deep inside. He is the only One who can unlock and uncover those deepest longings and bring them to completion. That's why hiding from Him is the worst decision we can make.

I tell my girls, "Tell me the truth. If you tell me, I can help you. We can work things out. If you keep it a secret, it will only get worse."

That's what God is saying to us, to you: "Don't hide. I'm the only way out. I am the only way."

My daughter likes to hide from me. Not the kind of hiding adults do, but the innocent, playful kind. It's frustrating, especially when we're getting ready to go somewhere and she won't respond when I call. But she seems to enjoy it just the same. One of her favorite places to hide is in the closet. I find her there often, sitting with her knees up against her chest, her hands covering her eyes. Even when I'm frustrated with her, I can't help but laugh when I find her. She always gives me a smiling look of astonishment and says, "How did you know where I was?"

I've tried to tell her that just because she can't see me doesn't mean I can't see her. So far, it hasn't made much difference in the way she hides.

Adults aren't any different, but the situations they hide from are much more serious.

How many times have you seen a guy driving a huge pickup truck that's pulling an even bigger boat, on his way to the lake, river, or ocean? He spends every weekend on the water.

Or the guy who disappears in the fall as soon as hunting season opens.

Or the woman who spends her time at the shopping mall, the manicurist, the spa.

Some guys enjoy hunting and fishing. And I know we have to take time for ourselves. But all too many men and women are hiding—hiding from their wives, their children, their husbands, themselves. And hiding from God.

Don't get me wrong. Recreation is fun. Spending a day on the lake with a nice boat, waterskiing, cooking meals on the grill is a fun way to spend a day. It's also a good place to avoid facing life.

We've gotten really good at finding places to hide—the golf course, the tennis court, the lake, the shopping mall.

Think of it: Hiding on a golf course is just like the little child who thinks she's hiding from her mother by covering her eyes.

What we're really saying is, "God, if I can't see you, you can't see me."

But you can't hide from God. You can't hide from Him by ducking behind your spouse's faith. You can't hide from Him behind the faith of your parents. Recreation won't conceal you or substitute for what He has to offer. God wants *you*. And to gain access to your life, He wants to strip away all those hiding places. That stripping away begins with an invitation to repentance. It's the one step in the process you have to take; you have to yield to His prompting.

Your mother can't do it for you. Your father can't do it for you. Your spouse can't. This is something you have to do.

Open your mouth and say, "Yes, Lord."

I had strained to be satisfied with love from other people in my life but had come up feeling empty. I wanted something lasting and life-changing, something real. This message of love resonated in my soul. That evening as the speaker prayed aloud, I prayed along with him. I asked Jesus to give me his love and heal my broken heart. I told Jesus I would follow him if he would show me where to go.

Almost immediately I felt different.

—HEATHER MERCER,

PRISONERS OF HOPE

CHAPTER 5

IN AN INSTANT

I tell you the truth, today you will be with me in paradise.

—JESUS OF NAZARETH, LUKE 23:43

The turning of repentance is instantaneous. There is simplicity in the repentance that leads to conversion, a simplicity that often eludes us today. We live in a society that has lost all sense of how straightforward life can be. Everything is complex, and if it's not, we find a way to make it that way.

A friend told me about watching C-SPAN the other night. They were showing a hearing before a Senate subcommittee. After listening for a few minutes, he realized they were talking about an investigation that had been conducted by lawyers who worked for a government agency. The investigation had taken two years to complete and had been conducted five years ago. Here they were, delving into the details of that investigation—a two-year investigation to find out if a backup safety system was working at the time of a NASA launch. They'd taken two years to investigate and three years to talk about it. Think of all the pages and pages of reports that were written. He switched off the television and went to bed.

The federal government isn't the only thing that's become complex. Try building a new home or even building an addition to the home you already have. In most parts of the country you have to file reports and applications with a dozen agencies just to get a construction permit.

Or think of something as small as your DVD recorder. How many pages of instructions do you have to wade through just to find out how to record a program?

When personal computers were first introduced, one of the major selling points was how much simpler our lives would be with a computer to help. Computers haven't simplified our lives; they've complicated them! We connect to the internet through a wireless router in the living room. The printer is not really a printer; it's a device that prints, faxes, and copies all in one machine. All of that is tied to a family network that lets you share files and monitor the online activity of everyone in the house. That's not simple. That's complex. It may be better than what they did forty years ago, but it isn't simpler.

Some of you grew up in a day when you left your homes unlocked. The milkman delivered dairy products to your door. You knew the names of all your neighbors, and neighbors meant just about everyone in town. You didn't have to call ahead before dropping by someone's house, and if you came at mealtime, she'd be mad if you didn't stay and eat.

Life is complex. Your day is complex.

Think about a weekday morning in the typical household.

You awaken early to get the children off to school. That takes the coordination of a major military operation. Most mornings, just getting them out of bed is a major task. You get them dressed. Make them eat breakfast and brush their teeth. You get yourself ready. Find their books. Herd them toward the car. Stop to find the car keys and make sure you have your cell phone. (Cell phones. They're great, but you wouldn't need them if your life wasn't going in a thousand different directions at the speed of light.)

You make it through all of that, and you're only at the beginning of your day. After that, there's work for most of us. The job. Employment. I've been working since I was old enough to walk. I had my first paying job when I was twelve.

So, you get to work. Answer endless phone calls before midmorning. Read a ton of emails. Then you remember you have a husband, too, in addition to the kids. You can't recall seeing him during the morning rush, so you telephone him to see if he made it to work.

Oh, yeah. You kissed him as he left for the office. You vaguely remember it.

The complexity of our daily lives, the news we see and hear on television or read about in the newspaper—all the things vying for our time and attention leave us feeling like everything is complex. We anticipate complexity. We expect complexity.

Repentance isn't complex. It comes in an instant.

With this kind of repentance, you aren't solving all the problems in your life. You're turning toward the solution to those problems. The initial experience of repenting, of coming to a conversion experience with Jesus, isn't complicated. You're stepping from one kingdom to another. It's a huge move for your life, but it's a very simple step.

Ever visited a foreign country? You could be thousands of miles from home, in a land where people speak a language you've never heard before, but if you can get to the U.S. embassy, you can be in the United States in an instant. All you have to do is step from the street, through the front door, into the embassy compound, and you're there. That embassy is American territory. The U.S. Marines guard it. Foreign governments and foreign nationals can't come in there without U.S. permission. Get inside that compound and you're home.

If you were a citizen of that foreign country and wanted to defect, to renounce your citizenship in that country and become a citizen of the United States, you could transfer yourself from that foreign country to America simply by presenting yourself to the guard at the door or gate and making a simple declaration: "I would like to defect."

You could even make it simpler: "I defect."

Instantly, the door to the embassy would swing open and in one step you would be transported from the country you previously served to a new one.

That's what happens with repentance that leads to conversion. You are instantly transported from the kingdom of darkness to the kingdom of light. In less than a nanosecond, your allegiance is switched from the lord of darkness to the Lord of all creation.

Nothing complex. One simple turn. I don't care what you

heard in church, I don't care what you've always thought about it. Repenting is a simple thing. I'm not making this up.

As a preacher's daughter, much of my life has been spent in church. I've heard the Bible read, and I've read the Bible myself more than any other book. No matter how many times I read the Gospels, I am always astounded by the immediacy with which the twelve apostles responded to Jesus's call: "As Jesus was walking beside the Sea of Galilee, he saw two brothers, Simon called Peter and his brother Andrew. They were casting a net into the lake, for they were fishermen. 'Come, follow me,' Jesus said, 'and I will make you fishers of men.' At once they left their nets and followed him" (Matthew 4:18–20).

Think about it. They responded at once. No hesitation. No questions.

If I tell my daughter to get in the car, she'll toss me a hundred questions: "Where are we going? What are we going to do there? Do I know them? Is she the lady with the two boys? Can we play? I want my doll. Where's Papa today?"

And that's just the questions she asks between the kitchen and the van.

When Jesus called, the apostles answered with action. Their action, their response, changed the direction of their lives forever. One moment they were fishermen, the next they were part of a revolutionary group that sent the world spinning in a new direction.

That immediate response wasn't unique to Peter and Andrew. The same thing happened with James and John: "Going on from there, he saw two other brothers, James son of Zebedee and his brother John. They were in a boat with their father Zebedee, preparing their nets. Jesus called them, and immediately they left the boat and their father and followed him" (Matthew 4:21–22).

"Immediately." The apostles had their lives pointed in one direction, and in an instant they turned in the opposite.

Now, I know you're thinking there must have been more to the story than that. The writer just left some of it out. What we have is a summary of what really happened. Nine weeks of ground work went into it. Someone researched their backgrounds, came up with a list of prospects, checked their references. A team of experts put their houses under surveillance. Someone went to their place of employment. Someone else researched their credit rating.

That's the kind of complexity we anticipate. That's not what the Gospels portray.

Perhaps we have in the Gospels a summary of the event, a summary of a more lengthy conversation. If so, that would mean that everything included in that written account is crucial. And the point of the account is clear: Jesus called; they responded. And they responded immediately. They didn't wait around. They didn't ask questions. They put down what they were doing and went with Him.

When they got out of the boat and stood up from mending the net, they were transported instantly from the kingdom of darkness into the kingdom of light. They were transported from this world into the world to come.

That's the same call God makes to you. That's the same invitation He extends to you: "Will you turn from the life you've been living and follow me?" That is the question that takes you to the repentance that leads to conversion. It is so simple you can make that choice right now.

Jesus says: "Follow me."

Turn to Him now. Accept His gift to you. Turn to Him and say, "Yes, Lord."

My heart was pounding in my chest. I raised my hand along with a few other people. The pastor instructed the students to gather around and pray for those with their hands raised. Three students started praying for me. I just cried and cried. It was as if waves of heat were washing over me. I knew God was touching me. "It's a terrible sin," I told the students. But for the first time I felt I was forgiven.

—DAYNA CURRY,
PRISONERS OF HOPE

CHAPTER 6

AN INSTANT, LONG TIME COMING

Hey, this has been a ten-year overnight success story.

—TAYLOR HICKS

Repentance comes in an instant, but it may take some time getting to that moment.

Frank Parker, a real-estate broker in Alabama, not so jokingly describes his youth as a time "when I was out there building up my testimony."

Building up my testimony.

Powerful, gripping testimonies were very popular in the 1970s and 1980s. You probably heard a few—the member of a motorcycle gang who found the Lord somewhere along the road, or the drug addict who found Jesus through a friend. If you had a past and could tell it in vivid detail, you could get an audience.

Don't get me wrong. I'm not suggesting those testimonies weren't true. Nicky Cruz has a dramatic story about how he was transformed by the Lord from drug addict and gang member to believer. You can read about it in *The Cross and the Switchblade* and *Run Baby Run.*

Dramatic repentance and conversion stories were once very popular. You don't hear them much anymore. The reason we don't hear about those kinds of conversions is very simple: Most of the conduct those people were engaged in is no longer viewed as sin. Or if it's still seen as sin, we've become so desensitized to it we no longer see it as dramatic. If you watch prime-time television, you see a hundred shootings and stabbings each week. Drug addicts come into your living room every night; some of them are the most compelling characters in the television shows you watch. You identify with them. They often come out as the heroes in the story, the only genuine characters in the one-hour episodes. We like the down-and-out person, especially the one who knows he's down-and-out and isn't afraid to show it.

So we see this sort of thing all the time, and it doesn't affect us, or if it does, we see it as an "illness."

In most circles, Christian or otherwise, addiction to alcohol is thought of as a disease. We have research that indicates some people have a genetic proclivity for alcoholism, one that is passed from generation to generation. When they become addicted to alcohol, we don't think of them as sinful people, we think of them as sick. That may be the correct view. I don't know. I'm just telling you where we are.

Addiction to drugs is fast joining the ranks of the problems that are defined as illnesses. The only thing that makes some people uncomfortable with calling it an illness is that drug addicts tend to be involved in crime, some of it violent crime. Purse snatchings, shoplifting, home invasions, and armed robberies are very often linked to the perpetrator's addiction to some illegal substance. That makes people angry and afraid, which leaves them less inclined to think of drug use as an illness. Alcohol use, on the other hand, is something with which most people are acquainted.

All that to say sin ain't what it used to be.

The more popular way of discussing sin is to speak of it as a personal disposition or conduct that emanates from an emotional wound. That's the way it's discussed most often in popular Christian literature. That's not the way Scripture portrays it.

Scripture depicts sin as rebellion against God: "He who does what is sinful is of the devil, because the devil has been sinning from the beginning" (1 John 3:8).

When God looks at our planet, He sees a rebellious creation. It's true, we are a wounded creation, but those wounds are not the source of sin. They are a point through which Satan often gains access to our lives, but they are not the source of sin. Sin comes from Satan, and when we sin, we join him in his rebellion against God. When we sin, we align ourselves with the kingdom of darkness.

Jesus viewed people in one of two groups. Sheep and goats come to mind, but that doesn't really seem relevant to a society that no longer knows the difference between those two animals. Suffice it to say, He put people in two categories.

One group, the religious leadership of the day, He saw as evil, self-centered, and rebellious. They were more interested in gaining attention for themselves than in worshiping God, more interested in their positions of authority than in being servants. "They tie up heavy loads and put them on men's shoulders, but they themselves are not willing to lift a finger to move them" (Matthew 23:4). They were a group that knew the truth but refused to live from the truth they knew. And they refused to convey that truth. Jesus said, "Woe to you, teachers of the law and Pharisees, you hypocrites! You shut the kingdom of heaven in men's faces. You yourselves do not enter, nor will you let those enter who are trying to" (Matthew 23:13).

The other group—tax collectors, fishermen, and everyone else—He seems to have seen as wandering, disillusioned, and deceived. Sinful, yes, but also like the walking wounded, living under an oppressive regime, not capable of escape, desperately needing a way out. Mark wrote, "When Jesus landed and saw a large crowd, he had compassion on them, because they were like sheep without a shepherd" (Mark 6:34).

That's how Jesus related to the people who came to Him seeking healing: "She said to herself, 'If I only touch his cloak, I will be healed.' Jesus turned and saw her. 'Take heart, daughter,' he said, 'your faith has healed you' " (Matthew 9:21–22).

It is to that group that He extended an invitation, inviting them to Himself and to the rest and peace that comes from His presence: "Come to me, all you who are weary and burdened, and I will give you rest" (Matthew 11:28).

That's us. That's right where most of us live. We want to be strong and brave, powerful and courageous. We want to be victorious. In reality, we're staggering around, shell-shocked. For us, Jesus has a message of hope and release. When He looked back at that woman who was sure one touch of the hem of His robe would heal her, I think He smiled.

He sees you now. He's looking right at you. Turn around. You'll see that smile, too.

In the last chapter I told you repentance that leads to conversion comes in an instant. That's true. It does. When you ask God to take control of your life, He's there in that same moment. Before the words leave your lips, He's responding to your "yes" with His "yes." You move from your kingdom to His kingdom— the kingdom of God—it happens that fast. However, the way most of us live, it may take you years to find that moment.

The music business is famous for overnight success stories. Most of them were many years in the making. You may not be an Elvis fan, but if you looked at a timeline of his life, you'd see a man who worked almost every night from 1954 to 1956. Many of those nights were spent in some grubby places—school gyms, nightclubs, private parties, wherever he could find a place to sing. Then in 1956 he appeared on the *Ed Sullivan Show,* and there it happened. Overnight, he became famous around the world. People everywhere saw him burst onto the scene. Everyone saw the dramatic moment. They didn't see that it took him two years and a lot of struggle to get to that point.

Your life has brought you to this moment. Many things have transpired to bring you here. Perhaps when you look back, you see some glaring mistakes, some obvious moments of rebellion. Maybe you have a story like that of Nicky Cruz, trapped in a life of drug use and lawless living, or maybe you're like the member of a motorcycle gang, riding the highways in a carefree jaunt from one disgusting act to another. Or maybe you have just one thing that makes you so ashamed. Whether we call it rebellion or illness or wound, the question now isn't how you got here. Forget about the whys and hows for right now. You'll find answers to those questions as you move forward with God. The question for you right now is, "Will you turn to Jesus?" Will you accept the gift He's offering you, the gift of His presence?

Your life has brought you to this moment. You don't have to wait any longer. You can turn to Jesus right now. You can be transported from the kingdom of darkness to the kingdom of light this very instant.

Do it. For your own sake. For the sake of the kingdom. Do it.

So with a nice standard of living, professional recognition, church and community service, I began feeling satisfied in a worldly fashion. However, I still had the feeling that there had to be more to life than that. That empty feeling in my life, instead of being satisfied, just seemed to grow larger rather than smaller with each worldly accomplishment. To the point that frustration was the rule rather than the exception, and my lifelong desire for peace of mind seemed to be getting farther and farther away, when it should have been right around the corner.

—GUY JACKSON

CHAPTER 7

BUT WAIT!
THERE'S MORE!

There's got to be more to livin' than just waitin' to die.

—GARY S. PAXTON

It took me six months to get off my worldly throne and
arrive at the simple childlike attitude it takes
to experience the kingdom of God.

—GUY JACKSON

You probably don't know Guy Jackson. Unlike many of the stories to which I've referred, he isn't famous, he doesn't have a television show, and he doesn't have a book on the market.

Guy Jackson spent most of his adult career working as a sales engineer for major equipment manufacturers. Don't ask me what a sales engineer does. I could give you an answer, but I'd only be guessing. Whatever the job entails, Guy made a nice living at it. His family was comfortable. He could look forward to a comfortable retirement. On the outside, life was good.

But inside, he was dying.

The job that provided the lifestyle they all enjoyed was feeding the family, but it wasn't feeding Guy's soul. It wasn't feeding his spirit. It wasn't coming close to filling the emptiness in his heart.

There was no way it could.

One of the many messages we receive through the media is the one about how the "good life" is so great. The good life—a house with a huge mortgage, new cars and new-car loans, credit cards and credit-card bills. This message is delivered by people and institutions with a certain indicia of authority in our society, and so we tend to believe what they are saying is the objective truth. Not only that, most of what we hear about what makes life good comes from individuals who have a vested interest in keeping us trapped in that life. They need us working eighty hours a week and making lots of money so they can sell us a mortgage or a car loan or a multitude of consumer items we don't really need. They need us to buy them because that's how they make money. We work to earn it, so we can give it to them.

To keep that chain going, they feed us two things: reward and fear. Pleasure and pain, or at least the hope of pleasure and the threat of pain: If you buy their car, women will find you attractive, you'll be the envy of all your friends, and you will have attained the success you crave. If you don't buy their car, you're an unattractive loser. If you live in the right house, people will respect you, others will see what a great provider you are, and you'll be happy. If you don't live in that palatial homestead, your children will be ridiculed, your wife will have no friends, and your life will count for nothing.

If we'd give this "message" more than a passing thought, we'd realize its logic makes no sense. But we don't. In fact, there's a part of us that wants to believe it's all true.

So we roll out of bed each morning, still groggy and tired from the previous day, and stumble to the car. We blitz through the streets to the office, or the sales call, or the job site, all the while sucking on a cup of coffee and trying to stay alert.

Got to make that money. Got to keep that check coming. Can't let up. House, mortgage, car, school, doctor, dentist. Groceries, vacation, retirement. Everybody's counting on us. Like the gerbil on the spinning wheel, we have to keep the wheels turning, and we don't see a way to stop without causing even more pain and damage.

It's like one of those chain letters you receive in your email. Can't stop the chain. Ooh. Bad stuff will happen. Money really is a chain. Think of it. We've been conditioned to view money as something real, tangible, and with permanent value. But it's all just an illusion. An abstract illusion. You go to work. Your employer transfers some numbers to your account at a number repository we call a bank. A numbers bank. There's no currency in your branch bank. In fact, they work very hard to make sure there is as little currency there as possible. So you have numbers in a numbers bank. You go to the store to purchase something. When you pay, you transfer some of your numbers from the numbers bank to the store. The store transfers their numbers to the manufacturer. And then it all starts again.

Employers don't tell you they're paying you with numbers. They tell you they're paying you in money, a salary. They use those words to convey a sense of security. In reality, the whole thing is an illusion, a merry-go-round in the sky.

I'm not making this up. I'm just telling you what Jesus has already said: "Sell your possessions and give to the poor. Provide purses for yourselves that will not wear out, a treasure in heaven that will not be exhausted, where no thief comes near and no moth destroys. For where your treasure is, there your heart will be also" (Luke 12:33–34).

Don't get me wrong. I like to eat as much as the next person. But the notion that our economy deals in something of permanent value is just plain wrong.

Like many of you, Guy Jackson heard our culture's false message. He heard it, and he believed it. That lie took him a long way from God. No, he didn't commit apostasy. He knew who God was, knew a lot about Him, and he went to church every week. But in his personal life, in the priorities of his day, in the way he approached life, he was wandering in a land far away. As with most of us, he wouldn't call his life the prodigal life. He wasn't living riotously and spending his way through life, but he wasn't serving God, either.

Thankfully, Guy's story doesn't end there. He listened to the voice of the Holy Spirit, and he listened to what the Spirit said through the one person closest to him—his wife. He responded with the response that opened the way to a new life—he said yes to God. Yes to a life of obedience to Him, and no to a life of obedience to that erroneous message. He still worked as a sales engineer, but he was no longer a slave to the lifestyle he once thought so important. As a result, he became involved in sharing God's true message with those in his local congregation. Working first through leading classes designed to teach about the life in the Spirit, he went on to become ordained as a deacon. While serving as a deacon, he was exposed to prison ministry, a work he came to love. Not long after that, he became an ordained Eastern Orthodox priest. Today, he ministers in a hospice facility, helping people face the ultimate transition from this life to the life that is to come.

Stepping off the treadmill of life isn't a comfortable thing to do. Turning your back on what the world has to offer is not easy. It's not easy to walk away from a paying job for a future that seems uncertain. But you need to know, the certainty of employment is an illusion, and so is the apparent uncertainty of choosing another way.

God wants all of you. He wants you from the top of your head to the soles of your feet. He wants you from your credit rating all the way down to the change in your pocket. He won't quit until He gets it all. He will not be satisfied living with you while your checkbook holds veto power over your obedience to Him. He won't be satisfied playing second chair to your retirement account or the benefits your company might provide. As good as those things are, they are only good. God wants to give you the best. He wants to give you Himself. You must lay aside your trust in the present and lay aside your fear of the future. Lay it aside. Turn from it. And turn to Him.

As I drove out of Tom's driveway, the tears were flowing uncontrollably. There were no streetlights, no moonlight. The car headlights were flooding illumination before my eyes, but I was crying so hard it was like trying to swim underwater. I pulled to the side of the road not more than a hundred yards from the entrance to Tom's driveway, the tires sinking into soft mounds of pine needles.

I remember hoping that Tom and Gert wouldn't hear my sobbing, the only sound other than the chirping of crickets that penetrated the still of the night. With my face cupped in my hands, head leaning forward against the wheel, I forgot about machismo, about pretenses, about fears of being weak. And as I did, I began to experience a wonderful feeling of being released. Then came the strange sensation that water was not only running down my cheeks, but surging through my whole body as well, cleansing and cooling as it went. They weren't tears of sadness and remorse, nor of joy—but somehow, tears of relief.

And then I prayed my first real prayer, "God, I don't know how to find You, but I'm going to try! I'm not much the way I am now, but somehow I want to give myself to You." I didn't know how to say more, so I repeated over and over the words: Take me.

—CHARLES W. COLSON, *BORN AGAIN*

CHAPTER 8

DETOURS
AND U-TURNS

A Christian's first call is to step from the line of Cain into
the line of Abel.

—FRANCIS A. SCHAEFFER, *GENESIS IN SPACE AND TIME*

The irony of popular Christian thought is that much of what we're told in church and on television mirrors the world's message. Popular Christian teaching would lead us to the conclusion that repentance is a way to bring our lives around to satisfying our expectations. If we repent and serve God, everything will turn out "right." If we repent and are converted to faith in Him, we will have a successful and lucrative career, send our children to the best schools, and climb the ladder to the top.

You might as well know now—life with God may not be what you expected.

For example, Chuck Colson was a brilliant attorney. A graduate of Brown University, he received a law degree from George Washington University. His intellect and ability allowed him to create a successful legal practice with clients all across the country, and it took him to the heights of political power. As chief counsel to Richard Nixon, he had a seat at the table where decisions were made that shaped the second half of the twentieth century—and not merely a seat from which to watch. He participated in many of those decisions, working from an office next to the president's, an office perched at the pinnacle of power. But the brilliance that brought him to the top also took him to the depths of a national controversy, one that came to be known by a single word: Watergate.

By the time Richard Nixon left office in disgrace, Chuck Colson had come to know Jesus as Lord of his life, and he was an inmate in a federal prison. The once-successful attorney with a bright future, the political operative who had helped put together one of the largest landslide victories in presidential electoral history, was a convicted criminal.

Those were dark days, no doubt. I'm sure his family wondered what was going to happen to them. His criminal conviction meant he could no longer practice law. The firm he'd worked so hard to establish was in the hands of others. Neither he nor his family knew how things would turn out, but God did.

Far from being the end, prison became a doorway to the rest of Chuck Colson's life, a doorway that led to Jesus's presence in his life, and to his own personal wholeness. That doorway opened for him through an act of repentance, which not only saved him but opened that same opportunity to many others, men and women who might never have heard the gospel had it not been for the turn Colson's life took. The organization he later founded, Prison Fellowship Ministries, would not have existed if Chuck Colson had not repented—and gone to prison. Thousands of men and women across the country and around the world would have been lost in a prison system that offered them no hope, no future, no life. Because of events that transpired in Colson's life, because he heard the Holy Spirit and responded in repentance, many others have come to know the Lord. When Chuck Colson slipped the key of repentance into the lock on his heart, he allowed God to open the door of repentance for them as well.

When I think of Chuck Colson, I think of Saul of Tarsus. Their lives bear a striking resemblance.

Like Chuck, Saul was a brilliant man. Bright, young, ambitious, on his way to the top. Hardworking, energetic, devoted to the task at hand, sold out to the cause. That's a recipe for success, but one that carries with it a great vulnerability to excess.

One of the smartest men recorded in Scripture, Saul had been educated by the best and had a bright future before him. Still a young man when Jesus was executed, Saul no doubt heard about Jesus's ministry: accounts of healing and deliverance, reports that He'd made Himself out to be the Son of God. Then, after the crucifixion, he heard reports of Jesus's followers repeating these stories and even making claims that He'd been raised from the dead. What Saul heard, he didn't like. Those statements and reports flew in the face of all he'd come to hold dear in life. Very soon, he made it his mission not just to confront what he saw as heresy, not just to oppose it when he saw it, but to wipe out all who claimed to follow Jesus. It was a task he tackled with energy and enthusiasm.

Armed with warrants issued by Jewish authorities, sanctioned by the Sanhedrin, he set out for Damascus in search of members of the Way, the growing sect of Jews who believed Jesus was the Messiah. Saul planned to round up as many suspects as he could and haul them back to Jerusalem for trial. But something happened on the way to Damascus. You remember the story.

> As he neared Damascus on his journey, suddenly a light from heaven flashed around him. He fell to the ground and heard a voice say to him, "Saul, Saul, why do you persecute me?"
>
> "Who are you, Lord?" Saul asked.
>
> "I am Jesus, whom you are persecuting," he replied. "Now get up and go into the city, and you will be told what you must do." (Acts 9:3–6)

Brilliant light enveloped him, but Saul, now blind from the light, stumbled around in absolute darkness. Saul was zealous. He was eager. He was consumed with the mission. But he wasn't stupid. His life might have been headed in the wrong direction, but he still knew the voice of the Lord when he heard it.

And think of that voice: "Go into the city, and you will be told what you must do."

I'm sure Saul must have had a million questions. I would. What are You talking about? Where will this take me? I have a job waiting in Jerusalem. I've worked hard to cultivate all these relationships. I've built up all kinds of favors and points with the Sanhedrin. Those old guys owe me. They'll make me a member before long. I know it. And, hey, how am I going to eat, and where will I sleep tonight?

Somewhere in all of that I would have banged my head and

scraped my toes. I mean, the darkness of being blind is absolute. Saul couldn't see anything. Most of us would have been overwhelmed by it.

But not Saul. He staggered and stumbled his way into Damascus to the home of Judas, a man who lived on Straight Street.

Think about that for a minute. Judas. On Straight Street.

I don't know who Judas was. Scripture doesn't say. He might have been someone who rented a spare room to travelers for extra money. Perhaps that was his business. No one knows for sure. Saul never mentions him in any of his later writings, and Acts doesn't tell us anything more about him; but I think Judas was Saul's friend, someone he'd known before, perhaps the only person in Damascus who would have taken him in, in that condition. Maybe, maybe not. That's just what I think. Whoever he was, he gave Saul a place to stay and, presumably, something to eat.

Saul was on his way to persecute every Christian he could find, but when God confronted him, he knew in an instant the mission he'd begun was wrong. Dreadfully wrong. Imagine the searing guilt he must have felt. For the first time, he was able to see his life as Jesus saw it, and it wasn't pretty. Imagine, one of the smartest men in redemptive history could not see the truth of who he was until he was struck blind by the Holy Spirit.

Sight is so vital today. Think of what it must have meant back then. As far as I know, they had nothing comparable to the Braille writing system we have today. There was no hope of corrective surgery. No trained dogs to lead the way. To be blind in that day meant a person would be destitute, dependent on oth-

REIGN DOWN

ers the remainder of his life. And understand this, when Saul was sitting in that room at Judas's house in Damascus, he had no idea what was going to happen to him. He was blind, and for all he knew, he would remain blind the rest of his life.

And Saul's response? He prayed. He was not bitter. He was not angry. Instead, he called out to God. He repented. God called him, and Saul responded. Jesus appeared to him, pointing out the erroneous nature of his conduct and the error of his beliefs. Saul acknowledged his error and did as he was told. He went on to Damascus and waited to be shown what was next. No questions about the future. No questions about the fate of the career he'd planned. Not even any questions about whether he would see again. He went where he was told to go, and he waited.

The remainder of his life was determined by that one decision. God's grace restored Saul's physical sight, and God's love helped him continue to grow in his spiritual sight.

From Damascus, Saul's life followed a long and eventful path through Turkey, across Greece, and on to Rome. Some say he even traveled as far west as Spain. Along the way he endured storms, shipwrecks, and beatings. In the end, he was imprisoned, tried, and ultimately executed.

As I said, we don't get to determine the circumstances of our lives.

And what was the result of it all?

Saul became Paul. Christianity spread across the Roman Empire from Jerusalem to Rome and beyond. Through his work, the church grew from a small Jewish sect to a religion with an identity of its own. Much of what we understand about the meaning of Jesus's life, death, and resurrection comes from the

70

writings of Paul, formerly known as Saul of Tarsus. We read those writings today in the New Testament.

Chuck Colson was just one person. Saul of Tarsus was just one person. Each one repented and then lived a life of daily repentance.

Repentance, by its very nature, means you take your hands off the controls of your life. You can't repent and retain control over the nature of your circumstances. All you can do is say yes. Yes to a probing, searching encounter with the Holy Spirit, and yes to continually repenting.

Jesus offers you no guarantee that the details will turn out as you want. He does guarantee you the life God has planned for you. Like Saul of Tarsus, like Chuck Colson of Boston, Massachusetts, you may find the future more adventure filled than anything you ever thought possible.

That future begins with repentance.

As the days passed, our marriage became a prison. The abuse became worse. I felt alone, ashamed, and trapped. To keep up appearances, I attended church without him, struggling to make up excuses for why Joe wasn't there and to create explanations for the bruises on my arms and legs. My weight dropped dramatically, and my health began to deteriorate.

I wanted to turn to my parents, but that little girl who always knew her father could solve anything couldn't bear to see the pain and disappointment I knew they would feel if I told them what was happening. So, I kept quiet and did my best to endure.

—SHAWN-MARIE COLE

CHAPTER 9

TURNING POINT

The world's done shaking
The world's done shaking me down
—COLLECTIVE SOUL, "BETTER NOW"

As I mentioned earlier in this book, my father has been a pastor most of my life. All of my childhood was spent in and around church. I grew up knowing about God. But knowing about someone and living in an active relationship with that person are two different things. For much of my life, I didn't have a relationship with God.

During high school, I fell in love with a boy named Joe. He wasn't a Christian and, in fact, challenged everything I knew about God. As a result, I put what I knew about God on the back burner and did my best to please Joe. I loved him and wanted him to love me. As you might guess, we married soon after high school. Too late, I realized I had made a mistake.

For our honeymoon, we took a trip to Mexico. As we made our way to our room that first night, I said something that made Joe mad. In response, he shoved me down the steps. What should have been a night of bliss, a dream come true, turned into a nightmare.

As the days passed, our marriage became a prison. The abuse became worse. I felt alone, ashamed, and trapped. To keep up appearances, I attended church without him, struggling to make up excuses for why Joe wasn't there and to create explanations for the bruises on my arms and legs. My weight dropped dramatically, and my health began to deteriorate.

I wanted to turn to my parents, but that little girl who always knew her father could solve anything couldn't bear to see the pain and disappointment I knew they would feel if I told them what was happening. So I kept quiet and did my best to endure.

When the misery became too much to handle, I turned to alcohol. Coworkers were always eager to indulge in a drink after work, and I was never in a hurry to go home. Sometimes it helped me forget for a moment, but usually it just made me feel that much worse.

On the nights I did go home, I found myself alone in our apartment with no idea where my husband might be or when he would return. When he was away, I worried about what he might be doing, and then I worried about what would happen when he returned.

All the while, the abuse continued. If he was in a good mood, he only yelled at me. Sometimes, he locked me in the closet. Sometimes it was worse.

Finally, after two years, I'd had enough. I didn't take my marriage vow lightly then, and I certainly don't now, but I'd given all I had to give. I had to find a way out.

In my mind, the only way God would allow me to divorce Joe was if he was cheating on me. So, I began looking for evidence that he was having an affair. Evidence of that wasn't difficult to find. I bought a tape recorder and attached it to the telephone in the guest room. The same day I bought it, I recorded a phone call from him to another woman. They were arranging to meet later that evening. I had my way out, but even then I didn't turn to God.

After the divorce, I began dating around. I went out to bars on Fridays and Saturdays, lived the way I wanted to, then showed up in church on Sunday like a good daughter and acted as if nothing was wrong. Relationships came and went. I put on a happy face, but inside I was empty and cold.

A year later I met a man named David. He was different from the other guys I had dated, and I was soon madly in love. He had been married before and had two wonderful children. I adored them. Everything seemed perfect. We attended church together, and he encouraged me to seek out God's purpose for my life. I was still empty and cold inside, only not so much around him. I wanted things to work out.

As our relationship grew closer, I came to sense he wasn't being completely forthright about the details of his life. I couldn't pinpoint anything, but what he said and the details I knew didn't always add up. I didn't try to find out the truth; I didn't want to know, really. I just wanted things to work out—a husband who loved me, children who needed me. I wanted to put a nice coating on my life and move on. David proposed. We set a date for the wedding.

Two weeks before we were to be married, his former mother-in-law sent my father an email informing him that David was not yet divorced from her daughter. My world shattered all around me. But even then, I refused to give in. Everything about the relationship was built on a lie, but I didn't want to accept it. I was determined to prove I had not been duped once again. In spite of all my efforts, however, the relationship slipped through my fingers.

Once again I was alone and very lonely. In response, I decided I would never again be the victim of a relationship with a man. From then on, I would be in control of my life. I would do as I pleased, chart my own course, and live by my own terms.

More than ever, men became a means to an end. I dated to see what I could get out of them. When I got what I wanted, I moved on to someone else. I wanted nothing to do with a long-term relationship. Many nights I cried myself to sleep, but I never let anyone see the pain. The wall between me and the men in my life became a wall between me and everyone except my family. It also became a wall between me and God. For my parents' sake I still did my best to keep up appearances, but inside my heart became hard as stone.

In all of this, the one place I felt safe was around my father. I loved him, and I knew he loved me. I told myself God would honor my father's relationship with Him and I would be safe as long as I stayed near him.

Then in 2002 my father had a heart attack. Tests revealed six arteries around his heart were blocked. He was set for surgery. We all gathered at the hospital to be with him.

Late that evening, they wheeled him from recovery to a suite in the intensive-care unit. Family members took turns going back to see him. I waited to go last. As I peeked around the corner, I felt my stomach drop to the floor. There he was, lying flat on his back, hooked to a roomful of machines. His skin was gray, and he looked as if he was already dead.

I thought, *This can't be him. This can't be my dad. My father lights up the room when he walks in. He's the one who protects me. He's the one who comforts me. This can't be him.*

But it was. And he was facing the greatest challenge of his life. A challenge I knew could end it all. I wanted to run away and hide.

That night I saw two things.

As I confronted the possibility that my father might die, I saw before me a great, empty abyss. My mother and brother have always supported me, but right then I was facing the real possibility that my father might no longer be alive. If my father died, I was sure the little order left in my life would vanish.

The other thing I saw was the state of my own heart.

As my father endured heart surgery and lay there in the bed struggling to recover, I sensed the Holy Spirit examining my own heart. What I saw there was just as discomforting as the abyss that seemed to be my future. My heart was dirty, nasty, vile, and desecrated. The heart of a woman is meant for purity, love, tenderness, and creativity. I had made it a cold, lifeless, filthy place filled with nothing but the emptiness of a life lived only for myself.

All the way home that night I wrestled with those two images: a future without my father and the present condition of my life. By the time I reached home, I was ready to address both of those issues.

As the car rolled to a stop in the driveway, I threw open the door and crawled out onto the lawn. There on my knees, I stared up to the sky and cried out, "Lord, I am so sorry for what I'm doing. Please take control of my life." I raised my hands in the air. "All I am is yours. Use me. I am your vessel."

From that moment, things began to change. God moved through every area of my life—relationships, friends, job, church. How I spent my time after work. What I read and what I watched. The things I allowed to fill my mind. All of that changed. It wasn't always easy, and He is still confronting me, but many things about me changed right away. As He worked through these aspects of my life, the pain and desperation faded. Slowly the loneliness disappeared.

Three months later I met a man named Brian. Unlike other men I'd known, he loved the Lord with all his heart. We started dating, and we started seeking the Lord together. Far different from my other relationships, this one was grounded in truth and honesty. And it was grounded in a love for God. More than ever, I drew closer and closer to the Lord. God was gracious to me. Brian and I are now married and have two beautiful children.

A few years ago I was going through some of my things. I found a prayer my aunt had instructed me to write when I was twelve or thirteen years old. It was a prayer for my future husband. She suggested I write out this prayer, listing all the attributes I wanted in my spouse, and she told me I should pray for him each day. I wrote the prayer and even prayed it for a while, but before long that prayer was lost and forgotten in a thousand other things a thirteen-year-old might do. I forgot about that prayer, but God didn't. He remembered that prayer. He remembered it and the deepest longings of my heart. God revealed His answer to my prayer when Brian came into my life. Brian matched every characteristic I prayed for.

I'm not saying my life is perfect. Loving God, repenting, doesn't mean your life will turn out all sweet and nice. There are as many ragged edges to my life as there are to yours. I'm saying God could not grant the desires of my heart until I was ready to receive them. I was not ready to receive them until I repented of the way I was living. Until I turned to Him and said, "Yes, Lord," I was unable to receive the blessings that come from His presence in my life, and He was unable to give me more than His call to repent.

When I allowed Him to reign in my life, He rained down His presence. In an instant, I stepped from the kingdom of darkness to the kingdom of light—the place where He dwells.

If you give Him control of your life, if you let Him rule and reign, you can enter the blessing of His presence. He is giving you the gift of repentance. A gift that leads to the greatest Gift—Jesus, God present with us and in us and in our circumstances.

Repentance is a key to the kingdom. Place the key into the lock on your heart, and let Him enter. Let Him Reign Down mercy and grace in your life.

After Stevie put Jesus first in her life, she was on me about going to church. I raced on Sunday, and that was my excuse for not going. But I really did not want to face the music. Then a friend told us about a new church that held its meetings in a high school on Wednesday night—I lost my excuse. We went. Everything that pastor said seemed to be directed my way. God was getting my attention.

—DARRELL WALTRIP,
DARRELL WALTRIP: ONE-ON-ONE

CHAPTER 10

CONTAGIOUS REPENTANCE

The jailer brought them into his house and set a meal
before them, and the whole family was filled with joy,
because they had come to believe in God.

—ACTS OF THE APOSTLES

When my wife experienced the release of the Spirit
and her life took on an obvious attitude of peace
and love, it blew my mind.

—GUY JACKSON

R epentance is contagious.

If your children attend day care during the week, you know all about contagious illnesses. One kid with a runny nose on Monday, and the whole place has a fever by Friday. The next week everyone in your family has the bug. It spreads like wildfire, and there's always a kid in the class who has something you don't want.

Repentance and the transformation Jesus brings through His

presence are contagious, too. God starts with one person, and before you know it, He's working in the lives of every member of that person's family. The change He makes in your life, the wholeness He brings to you, is not something you will be able to hide. Others will see; others will know. The completion you experience will become a message to your family, your friends, your coworkers, and your neighbors.

Remember the jailer in Acts? That's what happened to him and his family.

Paul and Silas had been preaching in Philippi, a town in what is now northern Greece. Every day as they went to their meeting place to pray with other believers, they passed a slave girl who had a spirit by which she could tell the future. She was used by her owners as a fortune-teller. They made a lot of money from her. Each day, as Paul and Silas passed her, she called out, "These men are servants of the Most High God, who are telling you the way to be saved" (Acts 16:17).

One morning, Paul had enough. He turned to her and said, "In the name of Jesus Christ I command you to come out of her!" (Acts 16:18).

The spirit came out, and that was the end of her career as a fortune-teller.

As you might guess, her owners were furious. They grabbed Paul and Silas and took them to the center of town, where they were hauled before the magistrates. Before the day was over, Paul and Silas were whipped and thrown in jail.

That night, while lying in prison, they began to worship, singing hymns and praying. Suddenly, an earthquake struck the jail. The chains that held the prisoners captive fell away, and the cell door flew open. When the jailer heard the commotion, he rushed to see what had happened. When he arrived and saw the door, he was sure everyone had escaped. Under Roman law, he would be held personally liable for the loss. Knowing what awaited him and his family, he drew his sword to kill himself. Paul shouted to stop him and assured him everyone was still there.

"The jailer called for lights, rushed in and fell trembling before Paul and Silas. He then brought them out and asked, 'Sirs, what must I do to be saved?'

"They replied, 'Believe in the Lord Jesus, and you will be saved—you and your household' " (Acts 16:29–31).

This chapter began with a quote from Darrell Waltrip about a worship service that led him to repent. Like many of us, he would have rather been anywhere else in the world than church that day. It wasn't because he hated God. His parents took him to church as a child. He knew about God. He'd been to church many times and knew what to expect in a church service. He didn't hate God, he just didn't want to be bothered.

Knowing God, putting Him first in your life, is disruptive, especially if you've been living life without regard to Him. Darrell knew that living life under the lordship of Jesus would upset the order of things—his order. Life wouldn't be so comfortable anymore. He couldn't just go to the racetrack and act like everybody else and never think about it anymore. He couldn't do and act and say things the same way anymore. Not that he had to change on his own, but he had to allow the changes to take place. He knew repentance would change him. God's presence in his life would make him whole, make him complete, make him different; everyone would know what had happened to him. Knowing that, and knowing his friends, the thought of what would transpire was a little more than he felt like handling. But he knew what God was calling him to do.

He's thankful now he had someone to help him, someone who kept after him until he surrendered his life to Jesus. Someone who continually reminded him of God's call on his life. Someone, closer than a friend, who consistently and persistently prodded him to respond.

Darrell Waltrip is a well-known sports figure. He's a commentator for Fox Sports. He's a NASCAR champion. Even if you don't like NASCAR, you probably know who he is just from the television commercials he does. He conducts a weekly Bible study in his garage at his home outside Nashville, and he's on the board of directors for Motor Racing Outreach, a ministry that works with people in the sport of automobile racing. As a result, Darrell gets a lot of attention for his commitment to Christ. But Darrell Waltrip wasn't always the spiritual leader in his family.

Darrell came to know Jesus because of his wife.

Well before Darrell found Jesus and got serious about living under His lordship, his wife, Stevie, surrendered her life to God. She was the one who heard the voice of the Holy Spirit whispering through the confusion in their lives, and she was the one who led Darrell to a place where he could hear that same voice. The release, the peace, the transformation she found didn't just bring completion to her, but to her husband, her daughters, and her friends as well.

Dale Earnhardt was one of Stevie's friends.

A legendary driver, Earnhardt's reputation in the sport and among fans was surpassed only by that of Richard Petty. Dale won seven NASCAR season championships, owned multiple racing teams and a shop Darrell Waltrip dubbed the "Garage Mahal" for its size, and he had a hand in a number of other automobile and sports businesses.

Sometime after Stevie Waltrip led Darrell to a place of repentance and conversion, she began giving him a Bible verse for each race. As Darrell would climb into his racecar, she would tell him his verse for the day. It was a way of reminding him who he served and a way of blessing him. One day Dale Earnhardt saw her and asked her what she was doing. She told him. He smiled and said, "You got a verse for me?"

So Stevie added Dale to her prerace routine and gave him a verse, too.

In February 2001 Dale Earnhardt prepared to climb into his black racecar for the season's first race, the Daytona 500. As he did, Stevie gave him a verse: "The name of the LORD is a strong tower; the righteous run to it and are safe" (Proverbs 18:10).

Three hours later, the race wound down to the final laps. Darrell's younger brother, Mike, was in the lead. Dale's son was in second place. Dale, the owner of both of those cars, was behind them in third place, blocking everyone who tried to pass him. The entire field was gathered behind him in a tight, anxious wad. Coming through the last turn of the last lap of the race, another car touched the fender of Dale's car. In an instant, his car veered sharply to the right and crashed head-on into the concrete retaining wall that lined the outside of the track. In less time than it took for you to read this paragraph, Dale Earnhardt was dead.

I don't know what he was thinking about as he saw that wall coming toward him, but I like to think he heard the words of that verse Stevie Waltrip gave him that morning: "The name of the LORD is a strong tower; the righteous run to it and are safe."

Those were the last words of Scripture he heard. They came to him from a friend who found Jesus and wasn't ashamed to share Him with those she knew. That friend was Stevie Waltrip, a woman touched by grace and a woman through whom grace flowed to those around her.

Repentance opens the door to God's work in your life. And from you, He is able to reach out to all those around you. Your life depends on your finding a place where you can repent and allow God's grace to redeem you. The lives of your family and friends depend on it, too.

Now it's time to take down the idols,
The statues and monuments I've built.
Monuments to the lies
Told to me by the one I used to serve.
It's time to repent of those
As well.

CHAPTER 11

A LIFESTYLE

We have the illusion that mere time cancels sin.

—C. S. LEWIS, *THE PROBLEM OF PAIN*

After repentance comes . . . repentance.

Most people think of repentance as the end. You used to live life one way, God confronted you, and you repented; you changed. That's how we're conditioned to think of repentance. That's how repentance has been presented in most churches. In your heart, in your own life, you know that's not the way it is.

Tracy is a successful attorney. He went to law school, studied hard, graduated near the top of his class, and became a trial lawyer. Was that the end of his learning? Of course not. He learns with every new case he takes. Over time, he's learned the law as it applies to many areas, but each case has its own set of facts and circumstances, which means the law that applies to the details of each of those cases is different. Practicing law is a life of learning the law and applying the law over and over in a cycle that keeps law clerks and publishing companies in business, finding and reporting appellate-court decisions.

Your own profession or occupation is much the same.

Tony is a mechanic at a local garage. He started working on cars in the 1960s. That served him well for working with the 1960s models, but what about now? Things have changed. New cars have been introduced each year. Fuel injection, sensors, computers—things have changed. Tony started learning about cars because he enjoyed driving them and working on them. That love of automobiles naturally led him into the automotive-repair business, but he would be out of business if he didn't continue to learn about them each day. He learns and applies in a cycle of learning and applying. If he tried to repair the latest Honda with something he learned from a 1956 Chevrolet Bel Air, he'd have a tough time making a living.

Life with God is much the same.

Repentance got you started—it opened the door to a new life. But it's not the end. It's only the beginning. Repentance will take you deeper into yourself, and deeper into God, than you ever imagined possible. This isn't an option that applies just to the "spiritual" people. This isn't something reserved for the serious-minded practitioner of religion. In fact, it isn't for the religious at all.

Religion won't take you into a life of repentance. Only the Holy Spirit can invite you there. Religion can't equip you for the stripping down of life that will happen on this path. To go where the life of repentance takes you, you'll have to find some courage you don't have right now.

You remember the apostle Peter. Brave, boisterous, always-first Peter. That same Peter, whom Jesus asked, " 'Who do you say I am?'

"Simon Peter answered, 'You are the Christ, the Son of the living God' " (Matthew 16:15–16).

That was heady stuff. In the hands of Jewish authorities Peter's answer would have been enough to condemn him to death. His answer equated Jesus with God. Among Jews, that was heresy of the first order. Not only that—he was proclaiming Jesus as the Messiah, the fulfillment of ancient prophecy. If he avoided being tried for heresy by the Jews, he could easily find himself before Roman authorities on charges of treason. Popular understanding of Jewish prophecies about the Messiah saw Him as a political figure, one who was coming to free Israel from the grip of Roman rule. Aligning himself with that view, proclaiming Jesus as the Messiah, the Christ, would make Peter an outlaw of the Roman Empire.

Heady stuff, indeed.

And so it is a striking contrast to hear that same Peter giving a very different answer the night Jesus was arrested by Roman soldiers and tried by the Sanhedrin. Way out in Caesarea Philippi, when Jesus asked the question, Peter had been bold and brave, decisive and unafraid. Now, he stood just outside the door of the hall where Jesus was on trial for His life. Peter could hear their voices, angry voices making terrible threats. Powerful men were arrayed against Jesus. Things didn't seem so clear anymore. Circumstances were different. Peter found himself face-to-face with Jesus's accusers—and the nature of his own soul.

Peter didn't realize it just then, but God was standing there right beside him, pointing to the door of Peter's heart, the source of his fear. But to Peter it didn't look as though God was there at all.

Now Peter was sitting out in the courtyard, and a servant girl came to him. "You also were with Jesus of Galilee," she said.

But he denied it before them all. "I don't know what you're talking about," he said.

Then he went out to the gateway, where another girl saw him and said to the people there, "This fellow was with Jesus of Nazareth."

He denied it again, with an oath: "I don't know the man!"

After a little while, those standing there went up to Peter and said, "Surely you are one of them, for your accent gives you away."

Then he began to call down curses on himself and he swore to them, "I don't know the man!" (Matthew 26:69–74)

Not once, not twice, but three times Peter gave an answer to them that was just as clear, just as concise, just as unequivocal as the courageous answer he'd given Jesus a few weeks earlier. This time, though, he changed his story. This time, he denied ever knowing the man they called Jesus.

That was a dark night. God was intervening on behalf of His creation. He was about to open the way for all creation to return to Him. Powerful forces opposed that move.

The future of the church was in question. Judas's betrayal had rocked the disciples. Of the twelve whom Jesus had hand-picked to deliver the good news of the kingdom to the entire world, all but Peter had ducked for cover at the first sign of trouble in the Garden of Gethsemane. Not Peter, brave Peter. His reaction wasn't to run. His reaction was to fight. Swift as lightning, he drew a sword. Who knew he even had one with him? Was it his? Maybe he snatched it from the soldier's scabbard. Drew one of their swords to use against them. That would be just like him.

Then a few hours later, he was there, lingering around the edges of a fight that was no longer his, hearing things he didn't want to hear, and saying things he never should have said.

Jesus knew this was going to happen. He knew what Peter would do, how Peter's own bravery, a quality everyone admired, would take him too close to the raw, ugly reality of the moment, too close to a scene that was beyond his control. The other ten needed him. Jesus needed him. More than anything else Peter desperately needed Jesus.

And so He'd said to him earlier, "Simon, Simon, Satan has asked to sift you as wheat. But I have prayed for you, Simon, that your faith may not fail. And when you have turned back, strengthen your brothers" (Luke 22:31–32).

If all Peter had was one shot at repentance, one shot at turning, what he said that night in the courtyard after Jesus was arrested would have ended all hope for him. That would have been it for Peter. But that wasn't it. Jesus knew his heart. He knew Peter loved Him, and He knew why Peter said those things and acted that way. And He wasn't willing to leave Peter there in the agony of those moments that night in the courtyard. He wasn't willing to leave him in the grip of the fear that caused him to respond the way he did.

Jesus was after Peter—all the way, no holds barred.

And He's after you, too.

One of the ways He brings things to the surface is through stress. Much has been said and written about stress. You can take courses in the causes of stress. There are people who will teach you techniques to help you manage stress. You can attend classes and read books about eliminating stress from your life. But you won't find many books or classes on how to allow God to use stress to show you where you need to grow, to show you things of which you need to repent. There isn't much out there on the subject, but it's true—God will use the stress in your life to show you what He wants to address, if you let Him.

Peter was feeling the stress that night. Stress brought the ugly things in his life to the surface, right where God wanted them, right where they had to be for God and Peter to deal with them.

Mike used to be a counselor for Teen Challenge, a program for drug addicts and alcoholics that addresses substance abuse and addiction through discipleship. He and another counselor worked with twelve men ranging in age from sixteen to forty-five. (The "teen" part of the name is a misnomer that harkens back to the beginning of the program. They work with all ages.)

At some point in the program, the counselors take their group of guys from the relative comfort of their homes and lead them on a camping trip. This is not just a leisurely hike through the woods. This is stress camping. They take them out for ten days, give them half enough food to fill them up, hike them twice as far as they think they can go, make them sleep on the ground under a makeshift tent that's really just a heavy sheet of plastic. From what I hear, it doesn't take long to find out who has which issues.

If you allow Him, God will use the stress in your life to do the same. But you have to be willing to cooperate, and you have to listen. He ordered the circumstances of world history for just the right moment for Jesus to come. He can order the circumstances of your life, not only to accomplish the broader purposes He has for you, but also to show you areas of your life He wants to address, to show you the people and things you've put in His place.

Repentance that leads to salvation is just the beginning of a life of repentance. As I said before, it's a life that takes you deeper into yourself and deeper into God. It's a journey to the wholeness of who God intends you to be.

The gift of repentance takes you to the Gift: Jesus, God present with us and in us and through us. He's standing there beside you, pointing to a doorway in your heart. He wants to unlock that door and enter that room. He's handing you the key of repentance. Slip it into the lock on your heart, and let Him in.

I just went on and on. I was taking amphetamines by the handful, literally, and barbiturates by the handful too, not to sleep but just to stop the shaking from the amphetamines. I was canceling shows and recording dates, and when I did manage to show up, I couldn't sing because my throat was too dried out from the pills. My weight was down to 155 pounds on a six-foot, one-and-a-half-inch frame. I was in and out of jails, hospitals, car wrecks. I was a walking vision of death, and that's exactly how I felt. I was scraping the filthy bottom of the barrel of life.

By early October 1967, I'd had enough. I hadn't slept or eaten in days, and there was nothing left of me. J.R. was just a distant memory. Whatever I'd become in his place, it felt barely human. I never wanted to see another dawn. I had wasted my life. I had drifted so far away from God and every stabilizing force in my life that I felt there was no hope for me.

I knew what to do. I'd go into Nickajack Cave, on the Tennessee River just north of Chattanooga, and let God take me from this earth and put me wherever He puts people like me.

—JOHNNY CASH, *CASH*

CHAPTER 12

STARTING WITH
THE BIG STUFF

I went down, down, down,

And the flames went higher.

—JUNE CARTER AND MERLE KILGORE, "RING OF FIRE"

G od goes after the big stuff first.

Right or wrong, in our minds we create a list of sins. Actually, we make two lists—one for the big ones and one for the little ones. Having an affair with your neighbor's wife— that's a big one. Thinking about having an affair with your neighbor's wife—that's a little one. Consuming drugs for recreational purposes—big one. Downing fourteen cups of coffee before lunch for the caffeine—not even on the list.

Scripture tells us that all sin is the same to God, regardless of what it might be. Murder is the same as lust. Lust is the same as pride. All of it is abhorrent to God.

But not all sin bears the same consequences in our daily existence. Thinking about having an affair with your neighbor's spouse might make you tense and irritable. It might get your face slapped by your own spouse if you stare too long while you're thinking. Actually having an affair with your neighbor's spouse will destroy your family and theirs. In some parts of the country it might just get you killed.

When Jesus comes into your life, He always starts at the top of the list—His list (and He has only one list!). What's at the top of His list might not correspond with what's at the top of your list, but frankly, you'll soon find out your list doesn't matter that much.

God wants your heart. All of it. To get that, He starts with the part of your life you value the most. Those life-controlling habits you hold so dear. For some of us, that is the only place He can begin. There isn't much else He can do without first shoveling out some of the garbage we pile into our lives. You know what I mean. Those things you start doing for pleasure (or treasure) that, before you know it, have control of you. Things that promise you a life of fun and happiness, only once you are really into them, you find out you can't control them. They control you. What you think will give you freedom and joy turns out to be a lock and chain. A lock and chain around your heart.

For some, that life-controlling habit is drugs. If you're addicted to drugs, God will have to start with that just to be able to communicate with you and keep you physically alive. Take a minute to do an online search for pictures of methamphetamine users. You'll see some pretty horrible things: skin lesions, rotten teeth, hollow cheeks, sunken eyes. The substance they're smoking or snorting or injecting into their bodies is sucking the life right out of them. Their lives are quite literally in danger.

Drug abuse isn't the only life-controlling habit.

Some of us are addicted to other things: pornography, sex. Yes, the human form is a lovely thing, and gazing upon it is . . . invigorating, to say the least. We are fearfully and wonderfully made. Human sexuality offers a powerful and intimate expression of love. But staring at pictures of it and watching movies that portray it is a cheap and demeaning substitute for the real and beautiful intimacy God intended. With each encounter you have with the substitutes, you not only fill your mind with images that will nag you the rest of your life, but you also fill your body with the rush of the experience, which only reinforces the habit and drives you further from the real thing.

Maybe you're addicted to shopping. Ever think of shopping as a life-controlling habit? Check your credit-card statements. See how many times you've been out buying "stuff." Not groceries, just "stuff." Check your closets, too. See if they aren't filled to the max with items that still have the tags on them. You might find enough in there to get through the next twelve months without buying another thing. Some of us could fill our entire Christmas gift list from the unopened boxes in the hall closet. America is the world's biggest consumer, and we all are out there doing our part. Those consumer goods manufactured in China end up in our homes and in our storage buildings. We have the consumer debt to prove it. Maybe you never thought of shopping as a life-controlling habit. Maybe you ought to take another look.

Maybe you're addicted to work. You might be one of those people I see in their cars, racing off to the office every morning, coffee cup on the dash, cell phone in hand, laptop open on the seat beside them. It makes my head tight just to think about it.

Life in an office can be life in a cage. Work, work, work. Not that laziness is an option, either. Some of us are just as addicted to not working. But work is no substitute for the fullness of the Spirit.

Life-controlling habits. Everyone has them. And here's some news: You have more than one.

Now, the reason God starts with the big things is simple: God does not like competition. So when He shows up in your life, He's coming after that thing that holds the attention you should be giving Him. Usually it's something rather obvious.

Once God gets a handle on the top issue, He starts on another, moving deeper into you, taking you deeper into Him.

And that's my point. Repentance isn't a once-in-a-lifetime event. It's a practice that recurs throughout the day, throughout the year, throughout your life. Repent and believe. Or, put another way, repent and change. God starts with you at one place, then works His way down through your life, through your soul, through the essence of who you are. At each turn He finds a door.

"What's in there?"

"Nothing," you reply.

Sometimes He'll smile at you. Sometimes He'll frown. "Let's take a look."

He hands you the key of repentance. You slip it into the lock on that door, and He steps inside. Around He goes through that room, pointing out the things you've hidden, showing you how they affect other areas of your life, questioning, confronting, bringing you to a point of change. When He finishes in that room, you move on to another. Down and down you go, deeper into you, deeper into Him. Unlocking the doors to the inner chambers of your heart, delving into the secrets you've stored there—the unbelief, the wrong belief, those things you've stuffed down and hidden away, the treasure that keeps your heart captive.

This chapter began with a quote from Johnny Cash. He's a good example of a life of repentance. If you read his books, you'll find that faith in Jesus was a central theme of his life from an early age. It just wasn't always at the top of the list. Many things competed for his attention—the rush of performing before live audiences, the artistic fulfillment he found in music, the pleasures success afforded, the excesses that came along with it. Somewhere along the way he started using amphetamines. Many in the entertainment industry fall into that trap. There's no excuse for it, but when you look at the way they live, it's easy to understand why they would fall victim to it. Being on the road is physically taxing; entertainers often work into the early hours of the morning and then sleep until noon, if at all. The schedule wears them out and disturbs their bodies' natural rhythms. It's easy to see why they would believe the person who says, "This stuff will help you." A pill to slow you down, another to wake you up.

At first the pills gave Johnny a lot of energy, but the energy amphetamines give is just energy they sap away from your body. Before long those tiny pills ruled his life. The experience opened his body to an appetite for the sensation the pills produced, a sensation he could never quite duplicate after the first few times he used them, which left him chasing something that was always a little out of reach. He took greater and greater quantities in an attempt to find that original sensation.

Until I read his book, I never knew he ended up in a cave, lying in total darkness, waiting to die. What a metaphor for where his life had taken him. What grace that led him from that cave, and from that darkness! Johnny had known Jesus; he just hadn't let Jesus have very much of his life. But he did that day.

The experiences he had that day in Nickajack Cave turned his life around. With the help of some good friends, he got off drugs. Still, even after he hit bottom, he struggled to stay drug free. Those appetites he'd created in his body lingered with him most of his life. He had to fight to get off the roller coaster, then fight to stay off. It was a constant battle.

Repent and change. Repent and change. Going deeper into God and deeper into himself.

You have something in your life that you wrestle with the same way. Everyone has habits. We're creatures of habit. When my husband gets up in the morning and prepares for work, he does the same thing every time. Not just shower, shave, and breakfast, but change in one pocket, keys in the other. I can tell the time by where he is in his morning routine. He says the same about me, but I don't always see it, which brings me to another point.

You might know about an obvious life-controlling habit, drugs or something else, but there are some others about which you are unaware. This process of repentance, this lifestyle of repentance, is a journey from the obvious to the obscure. It will take you to places in your heart and life you don't even know exist. You'll learn things about yourself you never before considered. That's where the work of wholeness really takes on power, down deep where you've hidden things away.

God calls you to repent not just once, but all your life. He wants repentance to be a lifestyle for you. Repent and believe. Repent and change. Take a journey down past the habit to the cause of the habit. Go past the outward conduct to the attitude and then to the underlying belief, the wrong belief that gives the habit a toehold in your life. Let God take you down to the hurt and shame you've buried deep in your soul. Down to the barren places, the incompleteness that has been with you since a time you remember long ago, and since a time you can't remember at all. Down past the things you do to the things you fail to do, the things you omit from your life—compassion and caring, feeding the hungry, reaching out to the poor and homeless—and the self-absorbed, self-centered attitude that lies beneath. You don't have to be afraid. God will go with you. He wants to reach those places because He wants to make you whole. He wants to make you complete. He wants to make you into the person He created you to be.

God already has pointed out something in your life He wants to address. He's standing right there beside you. The two of you are standing in the hallway of your life. There is a doorway at your elbow. He's pointing to it and asking a question: "What's in here?" Unwrap the gift He's given you. Place the key of repentance into the lock on your heart, and watch what unfolds before you.

Some of my friends told me that what I was doing was spiritual and professional suicide. They said that when people learned that I had been in a psychiatric institution, I would never be trusted again as a broadcaster or as a believer. I was sure that they were right, but I didn't need a public relations company at that moment. I needed a place to fall on my face before the throne of God and hear what He had to say.

—SHEILA WALSH,
THE HEARTACHE NO ONE SEES

CHAPTER 13

IT'S ALL BIG STUFF

Whoever can be trusted with very little
can also be trusted with much.

—JESUS, LUKE 16:10

It's all big stuff.

In the 1970s, a group of men with ties to the Nixon administration broke into the offices of the Democratic Party in the Watergate Building in Washington, DC. At the time, most people in the country had no idea what the Watergate was or where it was located. They soon would become well acquainted with it.

As the burglars made their way through the building, they placed a strip of tape over the bolt on the lock of a stairway door to hold it in the unlocked position. The only problem was they placed the tape horizontally instead of vertically; even with the door closed, ends of the tape were visible from the hallway.

A night watchman making his rounds saw the tape and removed it.

Some of what the burglars did in that building was never disclosed, but in the course of that particular evening they moved in and out of the building several times. When they passed through the doorway and found the tape had been removed, they replaced it. Once again they positioned the tape horizontally instead of vertically, which would have hidden it from view.

On his next round the night watchman saw the tape had been replaced. This time, he called the police.

Within minutes, police arrived. After a brief investigation, the intruders were located and arrested. Their arrest led to criminal charges and, eventually, a congressional inquiry. Trials and convictions followed. Before it was all over, many of those burglars were in prison, along with a number of White House officials, including Chuck Colson, about whom you read earlier.

Ultimately, the events that transpired in the Watergate Building that night culminated in the impeachment of Richard Nixon. Before he was tried on those charges, he resigned from the presidency of the United States.

Imagine the irony of that scenario. Richard Nixon's presidency was brought to an end by a piece of tape, not even a foot long, laid in the wrong direction on a door—twice.

Little things have a way of becoming huge.

Here's another one.

The September 11 terrorist attacks were horrific, yet they were not the first attempt to destroy the World Trade Center towers. In 1993, a man known as Ramzi Yousef tried to bring down the buildings using a van filled with explosives. His plan was to detonate the explosives underneath one of the towers in a way that would cause the building to topple to one side, sending it crashing into the other building, bringing them both to the ground.

The van he used was rented from an agency in New Jersey. That rental agency required a deposit before they would release the van. One of Yousef's associates went to the rental office, signed the necessary forms, provided the required deposit, and took possession of the van.

As you might expect, the van was destroyed when the explosives it contained were detonated in the basement parking garage a few floors beneath one of the Trade Center towers. The building was damaged, several levels of the parking garage were destroyed, and business there was disrupted for a number of weeks, but the building did not fall. It was later found to be structurally sound and continued in service. The van didn't fare quite as well. It lay in pieces beneath slabs of concrete.

A few days after the explosion, Ramzi Yousef was safely on the other side of the world, hiding in Pakistan. The man who'd rented the van was in New Jersey. Not willing to surrender the deposit, the man in New Jersey returned to the rental agency, reported the van stolen, and asked for the return of his deposit. Sensing something was wrong, the clerk at the rental agency told him to return the following day. In the meantime, the rental agency contacted the FBI.

When the man returned the following day to collect the deposit, he was arrested by the FBI. The case unraveled from there, and after a long, global manhunt, Ramzi Yousef was captured and returned to the United States. He now resides in a maximum-security prison somewhere in the central part of the country. His undoing came from an associate's fixation on a deposit of only a few hundred dollars.

Little things are never little.

When God takes the time to bring something to your attention, it's big. That thing, that issue He brings to your attention may seem small and insignificant at the time, but if He brings it up, you ignore it at your peril. Life, your life, may hang in the balance.

Those seemingly little things are portals through which God can reach the innermost parts of your heart. Down there, in the dark places of your heart, you will find the lies to which you've built many monuments in your life. Those lies are the things He's after.

Between this chapter and the previous one is a quote from Sheila Walsh telling about her decision to admit herself to a psychiatric facility. That's not a little thing. But she went there because of little things. They weren't little at the time, but they had started small and grown to unmanageable proportions.

That's the point. Little things have a way of becoming big, and when they do, you have to let God deal with them. Those otherwise little things are no longer little; they are clues, markers, showing you the path to the lies. Lies you believed long ago. Lies you agreed with, perhaps without even knowing why or what the consequences might be. Lies from which you need to repent.

A knock at the door that sends you cowering in the bathroom. A storm cloud, literally clouds in the sky and rain falling to the ground, that drowns you in a sense of guilt, guilt about something you can't even name, guilt that causes you to burst into tears of despair. Still, you know in your heart of hearts the Holy Spirit is prompting you, telling you something, only you can't figure out what it is, and all you want is to be in a place where you can hear Him.

Some of you can find that place on a walk alone. When I was in college, I found wonderful solitude at the mall. As an extrovert, I get energy, information, and stimulus from outside myself. Leave me in a room alone and I shut down. If I'm home alone, I turn on the television, not necessarily to watch a show, but to have the sound, the stimulus, in the room. So I went to the mall to be alone. People were everywhere around me, but I didn't know any of them. I was by myself with God, quiet, and peaceful, and yet surrounded by plenty of energy to keep my mind engaged. It was great.

Most of the time, we can find a safe place to be alone where we can hear the Holy Spirit and figure out what it is He's telling us in those seemingly small things that suddenly have become so big for us. But some of the things in our lives are so buried and obscured, so entwined in our memories and emotions that even the memories that might otherwise provide a clue to what's going on are themselves enmeshed in the struggle, the fear, the anxiety that makes the moment so large. At times like that, you need help. You need a friend, a counselor, someone to help you sort through things, someone to help you hear the voice of God. Finding that help is crucial. You can't ignore the need.

If God brings something to your attention, it's vital that you find out what He's saying—no matter what.

In that facility, Sheila began a journey back through her past to a point in time when she had been emotionally wounded. It wasn't something she'd forgotten. It wasn't some deep, dark memory she'd repressed, but rather an event she remembered but hadn't understood at the time. That wrong understanding told her a lie about herself, a lie that festered and grew and infected other areas of her sense of self. The trip she took back to that place was a trip taken through memories, attitudes, and beliefs. In another context, many of those memories and attitudes would have seemed insignificant in themselves. Yet, knit together, they were a trail from the despair she felt as an adult to the source of that despair, a source that lay many years behind her. She started that journey because she found herself no longer able to manage the circumstances of her life. Things that typically would have been small had become overwhelming. Using her memories and the aid of a friend, God was able to unwind her pain and set her on a path to wholeness.

When you begin a life of repentance, you may find yourself in a place like that. You may not admit yourself to a psychiatric unit, but you may find yourself reaching out for help in a way you never thought you would. Sharing your deepest thoughts with a trusted friend. Seeking the help of a professional counselor. Taking a retreat at a convent or monastery. Or, like Sheila Walsh, checking into a psychiatric unit.

No. You haven't lost your mind, but you hope to. You hope to exchange it for the mind of Christ.

Like the big, obvious, life-controlling habits, the little, insignificant things become huge in the hands of God. If He's pointing to something in your life, He's doing so for a purpose.

You don't know all of what God is doing in your life. So pay attention. If God is directing you to something, if He goes to the trouble of bringing it to the light, He's doing so for a reason. Your life depends on the work He is doing.

It's all big stuff.

Invite Him now to search you, to reach deep into your heart and into your mind. Call out to Him in the words of the psalmist, "Search me, O God, and know my heart; test me and know my anxious thoughts. See if there is any offensive way in me, and lead me in the way everlasting" (Psalm 139:23–24).

I stood before our congregation and wept. How could it have come to this? How did I lead them to this point?

We started with almost nothing, and from those meager beginnings God had been so faithful. Still, I wanted to be in control. I raised the money for the budget. I supervised program development. I hired the staff and saw to it they did exactly what I wanted them to do. In the process we'd used an attractive model to develop a very good church. A franchise. We were like a franchise store offering religious goods and services to the public. That's all. Worship was a show. Discipleship was incidental. God was not pleased, and I was the one responsible for it.

I stood before our congregation and repented.

—WALT KALLESTAD

CHAPTER 14

EVEN THE PREACHER

All to thee, my precious Savior,

I surrender all.

—JUDSON W. VAN DEVENTER, "I SURRENDER ALL"

The Lord can give. The Lord can take away.

I might be herding sheep next year.

—ELVIS PRESLEY

Jesus calls us to repent. That call to repentance is no respecter of persons. It reaches to those you might think of as obvious candidates and to those not so obvious.

When we think of repenting, most of us think of really bad sins. Not many of us would think of operating a church as being a sin. Even fewer would think it a sin to build and establish a church that had more than ten thousand members, an annual budget in the millions, and hundreds of new attendees each month. Most would think that was a good thing. My dad, Walt Kallestad, thought so, too.

Walt came from humble roots. His father grew up on a farm in Minnesota and learned about hard work very early in life.

Then, as an adult, his father sensed a call to ministry. He left his job, went to seminary, and became a pastor. Entrepreneurial faith runs deep in Walt's family.

After college Walt worked with various youth organizations and as youth director in several churches. Then, after a tragic accident threatened the life of his son, he began to take his relationship with God more seriously. He enrolled in seminary and pursued ordained ministry.

Following seminary Walt was called to a small church in Phoenix, Arizona. He arrived with little in financial assets and soon found the church in the same condition. Still, he worked at the tasks at hand, cultivated relationships, and did his best to do what he thought God would want.

As the church developed, Walt's competitive nature pushed him to succeed—new plans, a wider reach, a broader audience. With a program designed to attract attendance, the congregation grew. Soon they had expanded beyond the capacity of their building. Yet in spite of the success, Walt wasn't satisfied. Something about the church wasn't quite right, but he couldn't articulate it. A disquieted restlessness seemed to brood in his spirit.

With the church building operating at capacity, they decided to move to a new site. With a project in the works, Walt was soon immersed in the details of building, moving, and maintaining the ever-increasing church program. He ignored the unrest in his spirit and plunged headlong into the work at hand.

Growth in numbers continued. Programs expanded. Worship became more elaborate. The church hired professional musicians. Drums and an orchestra appeared on stage. At the same time, church staff grew. They expanded the day care, then added a preschool and an elementary school that will eventually include all twelve grades. Attendance pushed them to add more worship services. The annual budget grew along with everything else. Funding that budget took more and more time and energy.

Then in 2002 Walt had a heart attack. After surgery to restore six blocked arteries, he was forced to slow down. In the quiet of his living room, reclining in an easy chair, Walt was finally able to listen. The still, small voice of the Holy Spirit whispered, "This isn't what I want."

A few months later, Walt took a sabbatical. During that summer, he traveled to other churches, experienced new forms of worship, and listened intently to the Holy Spirit. In that process, he came to see the church he'd built for what it was: much of it an empire of his own making. What began as a labor of love had become an unsustainable retail outlet of spiritual goods and services. The success of that enterprise rested more on attracting new attendees than on developing committed disciples. Walt realized he'd worked hard to develop a good business, but Jesus's call isn't about developing buildings and programs. It isn't about raising budgets and handing out tasks to staff and volunteers. Discipleship is about building personal relationships, investing yourself in those relationships, and doing it in a way that allows Jesus to live through you. To do that, you have to become a servant. And that was the call Walt heard. God wanted a servant church—a church with a servant's heart, a church of disciples committed to making disciples. Not a retail church offering religious goods and services.

Building a congregation from a few hundred to more than

ten thousand is a phenomenal task. Transforming that congregation from an attractional model to a servant model is quite another. But Walt knew what he'd heard, and he knew it was from God.

When Walt laid his plan before the church staff, many rebelled. When he told them he wanted to move from worship as a performance about God to worship that was participatory *with* God, many of the worship leaders were hurt and upset. Not long after that, he reshaped the entire worship team. By the time the shift was complete, half his staff had been transitioned.

When he appeared before the church board, he had the outline of a resignation letter in mind. He told them what he'd heard from God—and what he was going to do about it—and suggested that if they disagreed, they should find a new pastor to lead them. He was tremendously encouraged when the entire board supported him.

A short time later he stood before the congregation. With the paid professional musicians and worship leaders gone, worship was led by a less-sensational team, but one whose hearts and music were fully surrendered to God. Not long after that, several hundred members moved to other churches down the street. Thousands of others left as well.

In the midst of this repentance storm, the Holy Spirit was there in power and in glory. Worship lost its glamour and found its soul. Spirit and truth came alive.

Repentance is a gift. Repentance moves you from the kingdom of darkness to the kingdom of God, from the rule of Satan to the rule of Jesus. When He reigns in your life, His presence pours out on you. His mercy and goodness rain down on you, bringing healing and wholeness. The call to repentance is an invitation to the life God has for you. Sometimes that call brings people together. Sometimes that call divides. Jesus said, "Do you think I came to bring peace on earth? No, I tell you, but division. From now on there will be five in one family divided against each other, three against two and two against three" (Luke 12:51–52).

When you get serious about knowing God and serving Him, some of your best friends may run for cover. People you thought would stand by you through anything may be the first to turn their backs on you. That can be tough. I know. I've been through it. But for those who abandon you, there are others who will come to your side. Many of those you find standing with you will be new faces, people you've never known, people you never expected to support you.

The journey to the life God wants for you is not always a smooth and easy ride. The journey of repentance doesn't take you along an easy path. Sometimes it can be quite painful. Still, Jesus asks you one question: "Will you open the door to your heart and let me in?"

Whether you're the mechanic at the garage or the pastor of the church, the question is the same. Say yes, and let Him Reign-Down in your life—reign over you, and rain down His grace and mercy as He pours out His presence.

Your wounds brought messages with them. Lots of messages. Somehow they all usually land in the same place. They had a similar theme. "You're worthless." "You're not a woman." "You're too much . . . and not enough." "You're a disappointment." "You are repulsive." On and on they go. Because they were delivered with such pain, they felt true. They pierced our hearts, and they seemed so true. So we accepted the message as fact. We embraced it as the verdict on us. . . .

The vows we made as children act like a deep-seated agreement with the message of our wounds. "Fine. If that's how it is, then that's how it is. I'll live my life in the following way. . . ." The vows we made acted like a kind of covenant with the messages that came with our deep wounds. Those childhood vows are very dangerous things. We must renounce them. Before we are entirely convinced that they aren't true, we must reject the message of our wounds. It's a way of unlocking the door to Jesus. Agreements lock the door from the inside. Renouncing the agreements unlocks the door to him.

—JOHN AND STASI ELDREDGE,
CAPTIVATING

CHAPTER 15

DANGEROUS VOWS

We, who with unveiled faces all reflect the Lord's glory,

are being transformed into his likeness

with ever-increasing glory,

which comes from the Lord, who is the Spirit.

—2 CORINTHIANS 3:18

A lifestyle of repentance is a journey to the sources of your pain.

I have a friend who struggles to control his weight. It's an issue he's wrestled with most of his adult life. He's not that much overweight. Just, overweight. This wasn't always a problem for him. When he graduated from high school, he weighed all of 145 pounds. The problem didn't become evident until a few years later, as he moved on through college and into adulthood.

Over the course of several years of repenting and changing, working through the issues one finds through living with God, he asked the Holy Spirit to show him the underlying cause of his weight problem. In an instant, he was transported back to a moment he remembered well but hadn't thought about for a long time. He was in the backyard of his childhood home, playing football with boys from the neighborhood. And he heard himself say, "I would give anything to be six foot six and weigh 295."

My friend was nine years old. Already it was evident he wasn't going to be that tall. And already he was making a vow. It was a vow he repeated more than once.

A vow is a powerful thing.

A vow can be the glue that binds a marriage through good times and bad, the force that keeps you honest when you're tempted to go in a different direction. Those are good vows.

There are also vows of a very different nature. Those are the vows that become monuments to the deceptions and lies we discussed earlier. They can even be monuments to a misperception we create based on events or circumstances.

My friend saw that football players were popular, strong, gifted. Deep down inside, my friend heard the lies: You aren't big enough. You weren't made right. Somebody messed up. God made a mistake. You have to fix it. If you fixed this problem, you'd be all right. Everything would work out for you. You'd be popular and powerful.

My friend heard those lies as a nine-year-old, and he believed them. Even at that young age he began building a monument to them. The monument was his body. It became an idol. And while he was building that monument, that idol, he made a vow to it. Then he worshiped it—with gluttony.

No, it didn't seem like gluttony at the time. He just ate more and spent a lot of time thinking about getting bigger. And he started exercising in the weight room. If he couldn't get taller, he could at least get bigger, more well-defined, muscular. Muscle mass increased, but so did his appetite. Slowly, gradually, imperceptibly, the appetite took control. Food, eating, promised him a way to get big and be a football player, to be something he felt he wasn't—popular, masculine, strong. It was a lie.

Lie upon lie, he believed them—and then it was too late. The appetite for food was in control.

You think I'm off base? Your spirit tells you I'm right. You've made similar vows yourself. Right now, the Holy Spirit is bringing those vows to mind.

Vows like the one my friend made are idolatrous. They're right there in your memory. You just need someone to open up the doors to those rooms in your heart where you've hidden them away. That someone is Jesus. You have to let Him show you the idols you've made, those desires you've put ahead of Him. He'll start by showing you the ungodly vows you made.

I'm not talking about wedding vows. Those are vows you make to God and to your spouse, vows God has ordained and consecrated. The vows I'm talking about are the vows you've made to the idols in your life. Don't go looking for the idols. Just let the Holy Spirit show you the vows you've made. Perhaps you made them yesterday or even today. Maybe you made them in the past and have long since forgotten them. Let Him show you those vows. The vows will take you to the idols, to the monuments you've built to the lies you were told, the lies you believed. And when He shows you those idols, you must renounce the vows and repent of worshiping the idol that arose from the lies.

This is the lifestyle of repentance. Books that talk about finding wholeness, about resolving conflict from your past, don't really talk about it in terms of repentance. As I mentioned earlier, *repent* is a word that brings a lot of baggage with it. Most people prefer to discuss this in terms of finding healing. Jesus talked about it in terms of adopting a lifestyle of turning and believing. Going deeper into yourself and deeper into God. Down there at the core is a belief, a wrong belief, that ties you to the idol. You have to get to that wrong belief, renounce it, repent of it, and replace it with correct belief.

When I first became a Christian, I never would have thought about vows I'd made as a child. Part of the reason is that no one was talking about that sort of thing. Even if they were, I wasn't ready to hear it then. There were plenty of other issues for God to work through. It took a while for me to understand this.

We've been talking about repenting and believing. Think of it in a different way. Think of it as repenting and worshiping. You repent and worship, only the act of worship is allowing God to take control of that area of your life to which He's pointing. You repent and worship Him by opening that area to His presence. Each time you do that, each time you say yes to His invitation, He gets more of you and you get more of Him. The work He does in your heart transforms you more and more into His likeness, changing you from one glory to the next.

Now, I know some of you are looking at your life and thinking, *This isn't so glorious.* Maybe not. Maybe your life isn't glorious because God is pointing to an issue you don't want to acknowledge, pointing to a door in your heart you don't want to open. I'm not suggesting that a lifestyle of repentance will smooth out every stressful moment in your life. In fact, as you saw in the previous chapter, embarking on a journey of repentance with Jesus may do just the opposite; it may add more stress to your life. Remember, this isn't about making you good, or making everyone around you good, or transforming your family into the image of perfection you have in your mind. This is about transforming you from dead to alive.

That transformation will take you to the vows you've made, vows you've made to the lies and misperceptions you believed, and the idols those lies and misperceptions led you to worship. God wants to tear down those idols. To do that, you have to let Him take you back to the place where it all began for you. You have to let Him take you back to the beginning. At each step along the way you have to place Him on the throne of your life. You have to allow Him to bring His presence to each of those places.

Jesus wants to uncover those vows you've made and the lies you once believed. Open the door to that room in your heart. Let the gift of His presence find full effect in your life.

"Woman, where are they? Has no one condemned you?"

"No one, sir," she said.

"Then neither do I condemn you," Jesus declared. "Go now and leave your life of sin."

—JESUS, WITH A WOMAN CAUGHT
IN ADULTERY, JOHN 8:10–11

CHAPTER 16

NO CONDEMNATION

If any one of you is without sin,

let him be the first to throw a stone at her.

—JOHN 8:7

Repentance is not about condemnation.

First of all, since we're talking about repentance, let me confess right here. I have a problem with the story about the woman caught in adultery. Why is it about the woman? It was adultery. If the woman was involved and the thing she did was adulterous, there must have been a man close by. Why not stone him, too? If what we're told about society back then is correct, that it was truly a male-dominated culture, she may have had little choice but to participate. Where's the man in all this?

Even as I wrote that paragraph, I heard the Holy Spirit saying, *There was a man, but I had John write the woman's side of the incident because I want you to know I understand what women go through.*

Jesus understands what men go through, too, but humanity has a long history of dishing it out to the women first. Accept it, guys. You've heaped a lot on us over the years.

But I digress once again.

Imagine Jesus, sitting there with the woman who'd been caught in adultery. I don't know if this was the first time she'd done this or not. The Bible doesn't say. All we know for sure is that she'd been caught with a man who wasn't her husband, and the crowd wanted her dead. Maybe some of Levi's neighbors were there. You remember Levi, the tax collector who invited Jesus over to his house for dinner, the man with the neighbors who had the long "don't" list. They were the people down the street who spent most of their time looking at other people's lives and very little time examining their own.

Whoever was in the crowd that day, they were serious about killing this woman. Why they didn't want to kill the man, I don't know. Maybe Jesus wondered the same thing.

How did it happen? How did it come to this? A woman caught with another man. One of them was married. Both of them were married. It didn't matter which. It was adultery, and she was caught.

Maybe she'd been working late on a project with a coworker. At first it was just work, but then one thing led to another. He mentioned an argument with his wife. She responded in a kind and understanding manner. To help him feel better about it, she told him about how her husband couldn't relate to their son. For some reason, he listened with a sympathetic ear and didn't try to give her all the right answers. Before they knew it, they were talking about things they should have never mentioned. Conversation flew past barriers that should have been respected. It wasn't long before they moved past conversation. Emotions and hormones were soon out of control.

For a while they were able to keep things secret, then it all began to unravel. His wife found a credit-card receipt on the dresser. Her husband heard a voice mail that didn't sound quite right. Then someone returned to the office building after hours and opened a door at an inopportune time.

Now it's not about two coworkers anymore. Families are on the line; children and futures are up in the air.

News like that can't be contained for long. Word spreads fast in an office. Coworkers gather to talk it over. Imagine them gathered around Jesus's desk. Everyone has something to say.

"I knew it."

"Yeah. I knew something wasn't right."

"You should fire her."

"They violated company policy."

Someone chuckles. "That's not all they violated."

A snicker flitters through the growing crowd. Someone in the back calls out, "Put her on the road."

Another retorts, "Her? What about him?"

"He works in another department."

"Same company."

"I don't know about him, but we can do something about her."

"I never liked her."

"She wouldn't even speak to me in the hall yesterday."

"Did you see her hair?"

"And that skirt. It was so tight I thought it would split."

"She's the reason we didn't get our bonus last quarter."

Everyone nods and murmurs.

"If she'd finished that project early, we would've made it."

"It wasn't due until next month."

"That's what I mean. They could have finished it last month, instead of . . . doing what they were doing."

"She always thought she was too good for this job."

"Now we see what she's really like."

They pause. A man in front catches Jesus's eye. "So, what's it going to be?"

While they've been talking, Jesus has been scribbling with a pen on a legal pad. Squares and circles. Lines and arrows. The room grows awkwardly quiet. After a moment, He lays the pen aside.

"You want to fire her?"

Everyone nods.

"She violated company policy. Put her on the road."

Jesus opens a desk drawer and takes out a preprinted form. He tosses it into a tray at the corner of His desk.

"All right." He points to the form. "That's an exit interview. Someone has to talk to her and tell her she no longer has a job here." He looks the man in the eye. "And you have to tell her why."

Several of the coworkers back away. The man in front scowls. "That's your job."

Jesus shakes His head. "You want her fired, you tell her why."

The man who'd spoken the loudest picks up the form. "All right. I'll do it. She deserves it. She destroyed a marriage. A family. Turned the office upside down. She gets what she deserves. If she ends up on the street, that's where she belongs."

As he turns to leave, Jesus calls after him, "Make sure she answers the last question."

The man stops and glances down at the form. A coworker leans over his shoulder. She reads the last question out loud. "Please rate the employee who conducted this interview. Was he/she courteous, fair, attentive, and helpful?"

The man's shoulders sag. He stares a moment longer, then tosses the form in the trash can.

Jesus isn't interested in beating you up for the things you've done. He's interested in rescuing you from them. Well-intentioned people fall victim to the deception of the Enemy. It happens every day. He catches you when you aren't watching, when you let down your guard, when you have your mind on something else. He sneaks up behind you and grabs you.

And, then again, sometimes you dive headfirst into whatever he's offering.

Either way, Jesus doesn't come after you to pile on guilt and condemnation. You can do a good job of that by yourself. Those voices you hear telling you Jesus isn't interested anymore, Jesus can't use you now that you've done this or that, those voices aren't the voice of the Holy Spirit, and they aren't the voice of truth.

More than anything, Jesus wants you to turn again—and keep moving. Repent and change. That's what He told the woman caught in adultery.

"Woman, where are they? Has no one condemned you?"

"No one, sir," she replied.

"Then neither do I condemn you," Jesus declared. "Go now and leave your life of sin" (John 8:10–11).

When I read those verses, I see Jesus smiling at her. A kind, understanding smile. The kind you see when someone is giving you a blessing, doing for you something you can't do for your-self, and being nice about it. That's what I see. A smile that re-leased that woman from everything the crowd had said about her. A smile that set her free, one that told her what they'd said wasn't the last word about her. What a message we need to hear! "I don't condemn you, either."

Most people want to concentrate on the rest of the verse: "Don't do it anymore." That's a phrase we've heard all our lives. Our parents said that to us when we were young.

"I'm sorry."

"That's okay. Just don't do it again."

If Jesus rescued you from the hands of a mob, told you He didn't condemn you, and sent you on your way, you wouldn't have any trouble with the "don't do it again" part. You'd be so separated from whatever it was you'd done that you wouldn't want to go back. For certain, there were consequences to that sin: families destroyed, lives in disarray, jobs lost, reputations ruined. But what you'd remember about that day would be the look in Jesus's eye and the kindness of His smile as He looked at you.

"I don't condemn you, either."

Concentrate on that image. Jesus smiling. Telling you with His eyes that you're not the person the crowd has said you are. You're not the person those voices in your head say you are. Yes, the accusation was true; you did it. Yes, the consequences for your behavior are real. But Jesus can see past the outward act. "Man looks at the outward appearance, but the LORD looks at the heart" (1 Samuel 16:7).

Jesus can see past the circumstances of your life, too. Past the pain and frustration. Past the lost family, the lost job, the ruined finances, the ruined reputation. He can see all the way down to the hurt that set you up for the fall you've just taken. He can see past the hurt to the lies you've believed. Beyond the lies to the rebellion. Past the rebellion to the heart He created for you. That heart, the one He wants to set free, lies at the very bottom of who you are, down in the deepest recesses. The door He wants to open is the door to the next room on your journey toward that deepest area.

Jesus offers you a gift. The gift is Himself. He wants to take Himself deeper into you than He's ever gone before. To do that, He needs you to fit the key of repentance into the lock on your heart and let Him inside. Use that key. Open the door. Repent and let Him inside.

The next day in my hotel room, reading my Bible, I came across a verse that exploded like the burst of fireworks from the night before—full of surprise and splendor: "God was reconciling the world to himself in Christ, not counting men's sins against them, and has committed to us the message of reconciliation."

That verse convicted me. It "outed" me. Oh, I wasn't having a secret homosexual affair. I wasn't picketing and protesting, waving a banner or carrying a big sign. But I had a big sign all right. I carried it in my hard heart, with the word "homosexual" scrawled across it. Every time I thought about my husband or my daughter, I held up my big card and waved my ugly sign. I counted that sin of homosexuality against them.

—NANCY HECHE,
THE TRUTH COMES OUT

CHAPTER 17

TRUE FREEDOM

The Pharisee stood up and prayed about himself: "God,
I thank you that I am not like other men—robbers,
evildoers, adulterers—or even like this tax collector."

—LUKE 18:11

Freedom is an intriguing concept. When you pursue it far enough, it turns back on you in a way that at first seems strange.

Think about it like this: Pick a topic or object of national significance that you hold dear—the flag, the Pledge of Allegiance, the Lincoln Memorial, our military.

Now, imagine your neighbor dragging that flag through the mud or burning it in protest. He's standing in the street and stomping it in a rage. Or imagine someone filing a claim in your local court or lodging a protest with the school board or with the principal at the school your child attends, challenging the inclusion of the phrase "under God" in the Pledge of Allegiance. Or think of someone spray painting graffiti on the beloved statue of Lincoln in Washington, DC. Or imagine someone taunting or jeering a soldier returning from combat.

It makes you so mad your blood boils.

Freedom, to be really free, means that your neighbor has a right to do those things we've just described. But that's not the end. You have a duty. You have a duty not just to resist the urge to interfere, not merely to refrain from punching someone in the nose, but a duty to defend your neighbor's right to do the thing that offends you and makes you so angry. In a republic such as ours, you have an obligation to stand between your neighbor and the mob while the neighbor protests by desecrating something you hold dear. In the political realm, that's freedom—freedom that is really free.

Hold that concept in your mind, because repentance takes you to a similar place. As we've said before, a lifestyle of repentance—repent and change, repent and worship, repent and believe—takes you deeper into yourself and deeper into God. Eventually, He will knock on a door to your heart that brings you face-to-face with attitudes—wrong attitudes, sinful attitudes—that are deeper than you've ever realized. When you travel far enough on that journey, you will come to a place where the Holy Spirit confronts sinful attitudes you hold against things that you rightly oppose—sinful attitudes you hold against sinful conduct. God wants those, too.

This chapter began with a quote from Nancy Heche. She is the mother of Anne Heche, an actress who, until just a few years ago, was living in a homosexual relationship.

Nancy Heche is a Christian. Not only that, she is Dr. Nancy Heche, a counselor with a pastoral-counseling practice. She was opposed to her daughter's relationship. She was so much against that lifestyle that she hated it. What began as indignation quickly became self-righteous indignation, and then it turned to bitterness and anger.

As a result, her relationship with her daughter became a roller coaster of talk, fight, estrangement. Talk, fight, estrangement. Finally, the Holy Spirit confronted Nancy.

Confrontation like that always comes as a surprise. We get so wrapped up in what we're opposing that we fail to see our own issues. Then, when we least expect it, God knocks on a door in our hearts, saying, "What's in here? Let's have a look."

Nancy Heche wasn't asked to lay aside her conviction about her daughter's lifestyle. What she was asked to give up was her attitude about that lifestyle. I'm not sure I could have wrapped my mind around that concept—being told that my attitude toward sin was sinful. That's a lot to grasp.

Many of the issues in our culture that confront us today evoke a similar attitude. We've all read news accounts of the opponents of abortion who so oppose it they hate it, hate the people who perform them, and hate those who have them. Hate it so much that they murder the doctors who perform abortions or blow up the clinic where abortions are performed.

If Satan can't convince you something is not sinful, he'll just get you to oppose it so much you loathe it. Loathe it so much you hate it. Hate it so much your hate turns to anger. Anger to rage. Rage to something tragic.

This is the place Saul of Tarsus found himself. He knew the law. He knew the commandments. Not just that, he was sold out to them. He was on guard for even the slightest hint of error. So when Christians said Jesus was the Son of God, it was more than Saul could stand. He loathed the very idea. He hated everyone who said those words, who thought those thoughts. He wanted to grab them and shove them into prison. He wanted to kill them. And that's what he did.

Regardless of which group you pick to hate, we all do the same thing. We don't kill their bodies. We kill something more serious. We kill their souls. We kill their future. But the future isn't ours. The future belongs to God. That's why we're forbidden to know it, except as He reveals it. Time, future time, is an area God has reserved for Himself. When we kill someone's future, we dabble in an area beyond our reach. Here's what I mean.

You remember the story Jesus told about the two men who were praying.

> *Two men went up to the temple to pray, one a Pharisee and the other a tax collector. The Pharisee stood up and prayed about himself: "God, I thank you that I am not like other men— robbers, evildoers, adulterers—or even like this tax collector. I fast twice a week and give a tenth of all I get."*
>
> *But the tax collector stood at a distance. He would not even look up to heaven, but beat his breast and said, "God, have mercy on me, a sinner."*
>
> *I tell you that this man, rather than the other, went home justified before God. For everyone who exalts himself will be humbled, and he who humbles himself will be exalted. (Luke 18:10–14)*

The Pharisee was so consumed with obeying the law that he gave a tithe on the herbs in his garden—one tenth to God. That would not have been a bad practice if it had been done in humility as an act of worship. Perhaps that's how he started, but then things changed. He began to look around and see others who didn't follow that practice. That made him feel good about himself. He was doing all right. God must be pleased. "I'm not like all these other folks I see."

And that's when righteousness became self-righteousness. That's when he began worshiping himself and not God. That's when he began to loathe those whom he perceived to be less than he.

We don't think of our righteous indignation as exalting ourselves, but that's what it is. Much of Christendom today, particularly evangelical Christendom, is more concerned with making sure people know they're going to hell than with making sure they understand how much Jesus loves them. Telling people they're wrong is just a backhanded way of telling them how right we are. We have become like that Pharisee, letting God know how good we are and how thankful we are that we aren't like all those others on our "big sins" list, and letting those others know how bad they are.

Then we go one step further. We shove those people on our big-sins list to one side. We make sure they know they aren't welcome among us. We quote Scripture about separating ourselves from sin, about coming out from among them and being holy. We shove some of those people we think of as "really bad" so far away we have no possibility of reaching out to them. That makes us feel good. We feel right about ourselves. We can swell up our chests, tip up our chins, and boast about how clean and pure we are because "those" people aren't any part of our fellowship. And that's where we shift over into God's business.

By shoving someone away from the church, away from us, we are really pushing ourselves away from them. We've moved so far from some groups that they have no possibility of listening to us, no possibility of hearing the gospel, no possibility of finding the kingdom.

Jesus had something to say about that: "You shut the kingdom of heaven in men's faces. You yourselves do not enter, nor will you let those enter who are trying to" (Matthew 23:13).

I'm talking about hating sin so much we ostracize the sinner and ourselves. Hating sin so much that we have no possibility of reaching out to those who are caught up in whatever lifestyle or practice it is we hate. It just may be that God brought up that issue you hate so much to guide you into a position from which you could reach out to those entangled in that same lifestyle or practice.

Are you against the gay and lesbian lifestyle? Why not get involved in leading a worship service that reaches out to those in that lifestyle? Perhaps that's your calling. You'll miss your call if you let yourself be satisfied with loathing the lifestyle, with hating it, with cutting yourself off from it. The ones you hate might miss knowing God, too. I'm not talking about compromising the gospel. I'm talking about letting God do a work so deep in your heart that He can set you free from your attitudes so that He can reign in you. Then He can rain down His mercy and grace through you to others.

Are you against abortion? Why not get involved with a group that counsels teenagers about their options? Or a group that works to reduce teenage pregnancy? Perhaps that's your calling. Jesus could change many lives that way.

You'll never find that calling until you repent of your attitude. God is knocking on the door of your heart, a door that leads to a sinful attitude you hold about a practice that is sinful. He wants that attitude. He wants to free you from it so He can use you to reach those around you who are caught up in that underlying practice to which you are so opposed.

He's knocking. Open the door and say yes to Him. Open the door and let Him Reign Down in your life and in the lives of those around you.

Although I was committed to following Jesus, I wanted to do it my way rather than His; I had given my life to Him, but I was still in control of it. As a result, although I knew and used the correct words and terminology, Jesus was not in fact Lord of my total life. Unwittingly, I had attempted to compartmentalize my relationship with Him, giving Him control of certain parts of me, yet not surrendering to His absolute Lordship. To put it another way, I wanted Jesus to be in my life, to be the engine, the power in my life, to be the motivator and the enabler who supplied the resources to do great things for God on earth and eventually take me to heaven, but I wanted to keep my hand on the controls.

In prison, I came to the end of Jim Bakker. God was teaching me that I must "die" daily and that the process would continue for the remainder of my life. The more I studied the Word of God, the more I realized that I have so much further to go . . . but I have made a start.

—JIM BAKKER, *I WAS WRONG*

CHAPTER 18

LETTING GO OF THE WHEEL

You can opt for God. Pitching every other plan,
you can opt for God.

—BETH MOORE, *GET OUT OF THAT PIT*

Please make a U-turn.

—FINEDRIVE GPS NAVIGATION SYSTEM

Take your hand off the wheel.

We are such an automobile society. While mass transit exists in most major cities across the country, life is designed with the automobile in mind. We have drive-thru banks, drive-thru restaurants, drive-thru hardware stores, drive-thru everything. You can eat lunch, mail a letter, transact banking business, visit the pharmacy, pay your utility bill, and pick up your children from school, all without leaving the front seat of your car.

Some of us love automobiles because we like machinery. Most of us are attached to them because they give us control. With an automobile, you can go anywhere, see anything, and do anything you want. Jump in the car and you can be in New York in a few days from almost anywhere in the country, a trip you can make all on your own. You don't need a reservation. You don't have to call ahead. You don't have to tell anyone where you're going. All on your own.

A friend of mine once attended a racecar driving school. Okay, I was trying to make it sound less masculine. In reality, it was a NASCAR stock-car racing school. I'm not a fan, but many people are. They have a big race in Phoenix twice a year. My parents like it, but then they like Harley Davidson motorcycles, too.

So, my friend's a big fan—that's NASCAR slang for a serious devotee—and he attended this driving school. Before they turned him loose on the track with the car by himself, he had to drive an instructor around for a few laps at full speed. It wasn't full speed for the car, but it was as fast as my friend could make it go.

As he was preparing to head out on the track that first time, the instructor gave him a few pointers. "When we get out there, I'm gonna reach over in front of you, grab the steering wheel, and move the car up next to the outside edge of the track. Whatever you do, don't take your hand off the wheel. I don't want to drive the car, I just want to show you how close you need to get to the retaining wall at the outside of the track."

He needn't have worried. I know the guy who was driving. Back then, he wasn't interested in surrendering control of anything.

We are taught from the time we can drive a car, "Don't take your hand off the wheel." American culture teaches us a lifestyle of control. No wonder we find it difficult to take our hands off the controls of our own lives.

Jesus tells us the opposite: "Whoever finds his life will lose it, and whoever loses his life for my sake will find it" (Matthew 10:39).

Let go of the controls.

The lifestyle of repentance and change is a lifestyle of surrender. It is a lifestyle of letting go of the controls and turning them over to God. Some of us have made such a mess of our lives, it ought not to be difficult to give Him a turn at the wheel. Still, for some of us, getting our hands off the controls sometimes requires peeling them off, one finger at a time.

You can resist God. Or you can cooperate. One way or the other He will have His way with you. You can surrender control, or He can take it from you. Either way, He wants to be in charge.

Jim Bakker found that out, but it was a painful process. He tried his best to serve God and retain control of the circumstances. It didn't work out so well. I'm not saying God sent him to prison so He could get control of Jim's life. But that's where Jim learned to let God have the wheel. Some of the circumstances in our lives are created by God. Some of them are created by our own choices and decisions. God gives us an option. We can allow Him to set those circumstances, or we can try to arrange them ourselves. The closer we get to letting Him do it, the better things turn out. The more we try to control, the worse it gets. Jim Bakker chose at crucial points to retain control over events in his life. A few of the people with whom he'd surrounded himself gave him poor advice. All of those things worked together to move him to the ultimate end: federal prison. I have to think God would have preferred for things to turn out differently, but when things turned out the way they did, He was right there with Jim, revealing Himself to Jim, revealing things about Jim to Jim.

God wants to be first in your life. He won't give up until He accomplishes that task, not because He's out to spoil your fun or destroy your life or send you to prison, but for the very opposite reason. He knows what's best for you, and He can only give you that best when you're ready to receive it. Receiving His best means surrendering control of your life to Him. Giving all of you, to all of Him. That surrendering comes through repentance—first the repentance that leads to conversion and then the lifestyle we've been talking about. Repent and believe. Repent and change. Repent and worship. That lifestyle will bring us again and again to the question of who is in control. God? Or you?

My husband is a graphic artist. He visualizes things very well. If he looks at a magazine, he notices right away if the corners for the advertisement boxes don't match up, or if the text doesn't flow correctly around a picture. I visualize things, but I don't notice things like that. I see pictures. When I think of an abstract concept, I immediately think of a picture.

We've been talking about repentance as a lifestyle. In doing that I've described it as a journey. When I hear those words, I don't see letters on a page. I see a man with a canvas bag slung over his shoulder, walking along a dirt road that takes him down a mountain. Right now, that road is following a gentle slope past a scrub oak, twisted and gnarled from clinging to a rocky mountain ledge. It's not too big, but just tall enough to cast some shade across the road. In the man's hand is a walking stick, and he walks at a deliberate pace. Not hurried, but deliberate, intentional. Up ahead of him I can see the road makes a sharp curve to the left and switches back on itself, going down still farther and disappearing beneath the canopy of lush, green trees ahead. I can see part of where the road will take him, but not much of it. Below him, past where the road disappears, a misty fog is rising. It looks cool and inviting. But there, near the top where he is now, it is hot and dry.

That's what I think of when I think of a journey. You might not think that way. I began this chapter talking about automobiles. I don't know much about cars, but they tell me there's a heavy coiled spring on the suspension of an automobile, something that helps the car ride smoothly and keeps the tires from bouncing too much. Think of the journey of repentance as traveling down the length of that coiled spring, moving round and round, making your way from the top down to the bottom. That's what we're talking about. Round and round. Down and down. Going deeper and deeper.

That journey begins when you give God control over the circumstances of your life.

If you remember the 1970s, think of a lifestyle of repentance as a journey down a Slinky. Your life is that coiled metal Slinky. Round and round you go, down and down. Deeper into yourself and deeper into God in a process of living that takes you through a cycle of repenting and changing. It's a cycle that repeats itself as you move down: Repent and change, repent and change.

God doesn't reveal everything about Himself in a moment. Thankfully, He doesn't reveal everything about you in a moment, either. He begins with us where we are, tackling the most controlling issues first, then moving deeper and deeper. This is not merely another event. Rather, it's a once-in-a-lifetime event that turned us in His direction. That turning sets us on a journey of similar events, a string of once-in-a-lifetime moments, a life-long process.

Taking your hands off the wheel, letting go of the controls of your life, doesn't mean no one is in control. It means *you* are no longer in control. And that's exactly what He wants. He wants to be in control. He wants to reign in your life.

Surrender control to God. Let Him reign. Let Him have control of the wheel. He knows where you need to go.

In the midst of my utter distress I heard God speak to my heart words of comfort: "I am a Redeemer. I redeem all things. I make all things new. Whatever you've lost I will restore. It doesn't matter what you've done. It doesn't matter what's happened to you. I can take all the hurt, the pain, and the scars. Not only can I heal them, but I can make them count for something."

—STORMIE OMARTIAN, *STORMIE*

CHAPTER 19

TRANSFORMATION

I will repay you for the years the locusts have eaten.

—JOEL 2:25

Eventually, I came to realize that God isn't a fixer,

he is a redeemer.

—PATSY CLAIRMONT, *I GREW UP LITTLE*

I will repay." It sounds too good to be true. Someone will actually make good on the mistakes I've made. The mess I've made of things isn't so big that God can't straighten it out. That is the antidote to the lies of hopelessness we've been told by the Enemy for far too long. Lies we've accepted. Lies we must reject.

Like Naomi and Ruth, we are searching for a kinsman redeemer. Like running home to a parent who can fix anything, that is where repentance brings us.

Sadly, too few of us have stories from our own lives that tap in to the notion of redeemer, redeemer kinsman, redeemer father, redeemer mother. Like Edmund in *The Lion, the Witch and the Wardrobe,* we find ourselves trapped in a dungeon at the White

Witch's castle. We believed the lie and ate the Turkish Delight, thinking we were so wise and shrewd. Then, too late, we saw the trap. Now all we can do is sit in the cold, shivering, staring at the stone figures around us that used to be alive, wondering when we will meet a similar fate. If only we could get to Aslan. If only we could find that Lion, wrap our arms around his neck, and tell him the awful tale of our lives. If we could just get to him, everything would be all right.

Like Frodo and his companions in *Lord of the Rings,* we're sitting in the Prancing Pony Tavern, the first stop of our journey, a trek that suddenly has become much more dangerous than we thought when we set out from home. We didn't know about the Ringwraiths, or the terrible power of the Ring. Now, we are farther from the shire than any of us have ever been, immersed in a world for which we are ill suited and poorly equipped. What have we gotten ourselves into? If we could just find Gandalf, perhaps all would be put right.

Thinking about these stories reminds me of my friend Joe. As a young boy, he used to walk home from school in the afternoons with his sisters. One day two older boys jumped out of the bushes to harass them. Joe was just a kid; the bullies were much older and bigger. But without thinking, Joe jumped in front of his sisters and whacked one of the big guys in the head with his metal lunch box. As you might expect, there was a fight. It didn't turn out so well, but like most fights, it didn't last long, either. The rest of the way home one thought kept rolling through Joe's mind: *When I get to my daddy, he'll straighten all of this out.* And he did.

This chapter began with a quote from Stormie Omartian, describing a word she received from the Lord: "I am a Redeemer. I redeem all things."

That's what God says to us: "I can take care of it. Give me all the hurt, the pain, the sorrow. Give me the mess you've made. Dump it right here in front of me. I'm gonna straighten everything out."

When I was a young girl, I sometimes got into trouble. I made mistakes. I didn't always make the best choices. But I knew one thing for certain: If I could just get to my father and tell him my troubles, he could straighten out everything. It might not be comfortable. I might be embarrassed to tell him what I'd done, but if I could just get to him, everything would turn out right. Maybe not the way I wanted things to go in the beginning, but it would turn out right.

Your life might be in a mess. I don't know what you've done. I don't have to know. You know all the decisions you've made. You know all the wrong choices you've made. God knows them, too. He wants you to bring all of that to Him and pour it out right there at His feet. He wants to redeem your life.

I'm not suggesting you can get to the same place you could have reached as a child. Options and opportunities of one age are not always available at a later age. But regardless of where life has taken you, God can make something incredible out of your future and the mistakes of your past.

That friend of mine I told you about earlier, the one who went to the racing school, dreamed as a teenager of being a racecar driver. No one else in his family was very interested in the sport, and so no one was around to encourage him in that direction. Still, it was a dream that never quite went away. Years later, while driving the racecar around the track at driving school, he realized he could have been successful as a driver—if he'd started when he was eighteen. By the time he attended that driving school, though, he was forty years old. That childhood dream was never going to come true. Maybe he wasn't supposed to be a racecar driver. I don't think he would swap anything about his life for that dream now. But my point is, there are things you can do if you start at eighteen that you can't get to at forty.

You see guys on television playing professional basketball. Most of those men started playing organized basketball when they were six or seven years old. The skills they have now are skills they've acquired over a lifetime of learning, learning that took them in a single direction. Dancers are the same. Most of them started taking dance lessons when they were three years old. At forty, you can't get off the couch and play professional basketball. You can't get off the couch at that age and dance as a professional, either. You can get off the couch and do something, but it's not going to be professional basketball or spinning across the stage with a professional dance company.

That may sound disappointing. Far from it. The neat thing about repentance is, it comes with a twist.

That friend of mine who wanted to be a racecar driver had other childhood dreams. Not long after he attended driving school and saw for himself that driving a racecar for a living wasn't going to happen, he got in touch with another childhood dream, a dream he'd guarded deep in the recesses of his heart, far deeper than any of the others: to be a writer.

Think of it like this.

By letting go of that boyhood dream of driving a racecar, he was actually putting the key of repentance into the lock on his heart. It didn't seem like repentance at the time. What was there to repent of? It was a boyhood dream. He'd moved on to a professional career. Why the need to repent? It seemed so silly, all this over a childhood dream.

Still, God kept pointing to a door in his heart. "Let's have a look in this room."

"Why? There's nothing in there."

"Let's have a look."

"I'm telling you, there's nothing in there. Just a kid's dream. A fantasy. I'm past all that now. In fact, I have to get to the office."

God smiled and nodded. "Let's have a look."

Finally, he slipped the key of repentance into the lock on his heart and opened the door to the room that held that dream of being a racecar driver. As he and God stepped inside, he saw for the first time how cluttered that room really was. The room of his heart that held that dream was cluttered with disappointment, frustration, and anger. Moving through the room of his heart, the Holy Spirit wiped all those things away. Buried beneath the boxes of anger, frustration, and disappointment was a beautiful antique trunk. It had been sitting in the center of that room all this time. Inside that trunk was the treasure of the other dream, the dream of being a writer, the dream he was born to fulfill. I'm glad God opened that area of his life because he's helping me with this book.

So there may be some things you passed by in life to which you can't return. Skills that could have been learned at one time that cannot be learned in the same way now. Relationships that were broken and destroyed and, though they can be redeemed now, won't ever be the relationship they would have been if things had gone differently. God will put your life together. It will be wonderful and exciting, and it will penetrate to the core of who you are, satisfying the deepest longings of your heart, longings and desires you've forgotten, longings and desires you never knew you had. But you aren't going back to the beginning to start over and live the past you wish you'd had. You're going on to something more marvelous than that.

I like to shop in antique stores. Not that I can afford to buy genuine antiques, but I like to look at them anyway. The beauty of an antique isn't in its spotless finish or its unmarred appearance. The beauty of an antique is in the rich luster it has acquired, a luster given to it by years of use. Lots of Sunday dinners were eaten on that dining table to give it that dark sheen. It's the patina that makes it so attractive. Refinish it and you will destroy its beauty and value.

Wholeness isn't about wiping away all the scars. It's about transforming those scars into something more beautiful than before. Those wounds deep in your heart will be healed. Some of the scars will disappear. What remains of who you used to be will be transformed into something more wonderful and more beautiful than ever before.

God is waiting. He wants to put your life back together. Nothing you've done is too big for Him to handle. He'll do this when you take a journey with Him, the journey we've been discussing, the journey of repentance. A lifestyle of repentance: repent and believe, repent and worship, repent and change. Let Him transform you. Let Him Reign Down.

Only a bad person needs to repent: only a good person can repent perfectly. The worse you are the more you need it and the less you can do it. The only person who could do it perfectly would be a perfect person—and he would not need it.

—C. S. LEWIS, *MERE CHRISTIANITY*

CHAPTER 20

RSVP REQUIRED

Seek the LORD while he may be found;

call on him while he is near.

—ISAIAH 55:6

I have revealed you to those whom you

gave me out of the world.

—JOHN 17:6

When the opportunity to repent comes your way, don't ignore it.

You can't get to God on your own. You come only by invitation. That invitation comes from the Holy Spirit.

The Queen of England travels in a cocoon. She lives in a cocoon. Everywhere she goes, there is a space around her in which no one is allowed to enter. She has guards with her to keep even the most innocent out of that space. She is royalty. Mere commoners, solely because they are commoners, aren't allowed to approach her or invade her personal space without an invitation.

You can't get there from here. Someone has to show you the way. Someone has to invite you.

Several years ago, friends of mine adopted a child from China. The application process was lengthy and required a small mountain of paperwork—birth certificates, marriage certificate, deed to their house—all of which had to be certified by various government officials both in the United States and in China. Using credit cards and FedEx, they were able to assemble the required information in just a few weeks. Everyone was amazed they could do it so quickly. The documents were bundled up and submitted to Chinese authorities. They reviewed everything and chose a child from an orphanage for my friends. News of that selection first came by fax, a referral document and grainy photograph of an infant staring at a camera. They were elated and ready to travel to get her. But they couldn't. They had to wait. I don't know what travel is like to China today, but back then you had to wait for an invitation. You couldn't go there on a whim. Someone had to invite you.

You can't get there from here. Someone has to invite you.

Most Protestants are so steeped in the notion of grace that we lose sight of the fact that grace is not something of our own doing. We didn't invent grace. We didn't create it. Grace is not our decision or our act. It is an act, an extension of unmerited favor, that emanates solely and only from the character of God. He is the author and dispenser of grace.

Think about these words of Jesus: "No one comes to the Father except through me" (John 14:6).

The way to God is fixed. It is immovable and unchangeable.

Listen to newscasts and interviews on television, and you will hear people talking about their religious beliefs as "my faith." A popular concept of God among us today presents Him as "my God." As if I have my god, and you have yours. I have my faith, and you have yours. Today, many think they can work out their own sense of the "religious other."

You might be able to construct for yourself a sense of religious self-validation, but you won't get to know the one true living God on your own. Holding some philosophical system of thought in your mind that you label "my faith" won't introduce you to a living, powerful, relationship with the Lord of heaven and earth, a relationship capable of bringing you into the wholeness and fullness for which you were created.

To get to that, to get to know Him—the one who created all that exists and wants to make you whole—you must have an invitation. He must invite you. That's why it's called grace. That's why it's called mercy. He must invite you. And He does.

Now the fact that He must—and does—invite you doesn't mean the thing is done. You must respond. You must not let the opportunity for repentance pass you by.

As a young girl in the classic story *Little Women,* Jo meets a boy named Laurie who lives next door with his grandfather. Jo is immediately infatuated with him, and Laurie with her. As time passes and they grow up, Jo and her sisters spend more and more time with him. Finally, as he approaches manhood, Laurie proposes to Jo. She has her heart set on the great, wide world and says no. Laurie persists, but Jo continues to refuse and eventually moves away to New York in hopes of pursuing a writing career. Time passes, she sees the world, and comes back home. Interested now in Laurie, she finds he is to marry her younger sister, with whom he developed a relationship in her absence.

Jo thought she was pushing Laurie away. In reality, she was pushing herself away. With each refusal of Laurie's overtures, she moved herself further and further from him. He hadn't moved. He was still there, at least at first, pursuing her, wooing her, trying to get her to change her mind. Then, perhaps subtly at first, she moved so far away she was out of the picture.

Or think of Tristan Ludlow in *Legends of the Fall*. He was pursued by Susannah Fincannon, who waited and waited. Still Tristan wandered the globe in search of one adventure after another in an attempt to block out the pain and anguish of his younger brother's death, a loss for which he felt responsible. At first, Susannah waited for him, but as time passed, he moved further and further away. Eventually Tristan returned, finally ready to settle down and get serious about life and Susannah, only to find she'd married his older brother, Alfred.

My point is this: You can say no only so many times. Each time you say no to God, you push yourself further and further from Him. You are the one who moves. He stays right where He's always been. Push yourself far enough away, and you'll be so far away from Him you can't get back.

I'm not making this up.

You remember how Moses went to Pharaoh to ask him to release the people of Israel from bondage. At first Pharaoh refused, saying, "Who is the LORD, that I should obey him and let Israel go? I do not know the LORD and I will not let Israel go" (Exodus 5:2).

Moses returned again and again. Several times Pharaoh rejected him out of hand, but a few times he entertained the notion of letting Israel go, then changed his mind. Each time, the Scripture says, "Pharaoh hardened his heart." He could see only the slaves, Moses, the bricks they were making, and the work they performed. Perhaps he was jealous of Moses; they'd known each other since childhood. Perhaps he was angry with Moses for not telling him that he was a Hebrew. For whatever reason, Pharaoh couldn't see what he was really doing. He couldn't see the One who really was making the request, and he couldn't see the effect on his own heart of continuing to refuse.

With each decision, with each refusal, Pharaoh moved himself further and further away from God. Each time Moses and Aaron appeared before Pharaoh, each time they asked for Israel to be released, God offered Pharaoh an opportunity. An opportunity to join Him in His redemptive work. An opportunity to save himself, his family, perhaps an opportunity for all of Egypt. But Pharaoh refused, and with each refusal he pushed himself further away from the possibility of returning.

Over and over, back and forth. Moses asked Pharaoh to let Israel go into the desert to worship. A few times, Pharaoh came close. He said yes when God sent a plague of frogs, then changed his mind. He said yes again when God sent the gnats, and again when He sent the flies, and the hail, only to change his mind at the last moment.

Finally there came a point when time had run out. God's purposes for Israel could be delayed no longer. He had to move forward. The time for repentance had passed. God stepped into Pharaoh's life, only this time it was not to offer repentance but to execute judgment.

With the plague of locusts, the story takes a dramatic turn. From that point, Scripture says, "The LORD hardened Pharaoh's heart" (Exodus 10:20).

The Lord hardened his heart. That's a dramatic move. At first, Pharaoh hardened his own heart. Then, God hardened it. By then, Pharaoh was as far from God as he could get. Only this time, the opportunities to repent had run out.

Think of it. Pharaoh saw things no one had ever seen before. He saw things no one has seen since. He watched as the Nile River turned to blood. Not only that, but all water in the entire country turned to blood—all the tributaries and creeks and even the water in the water jars. Pharaoh saw the blood. He smelled the stench as all the fish in the river died.

There was a plague of frogs, followed by gnats, then flies. Egyptian livestock died. Boils broke out on the skin of Egyptian men and animals. There was a hailstorm the likes of which no one had ever seen.

Some of Pharaoh's own men realized what was happening. When the swarm of gnats arose, his magicians told him, "This is the finger of God" (Exodus 8:19). When the hailstorm came, Scripture says, "Those officials of Pharaoh who feared the word of the LORD hurried to bring their slaves and their livestock inside" (Exodus 9:20). When the locusts devoured what the hail hadn't destroyed, some of those same people tried to warn him: "How long will this man be a snare to us? Let the people go, so that they may worship the LORD their God. Do you not yet realize that Egypt is ruined?" (Exodus 10:7).

Still, he would not repent.

And then came that terrible night when the firstborn of every Egyptian died. Someone died in every Egyptian family across the entire country. Someone died in a house a few blocks away. Someone died in the house across the street. Someone died in Pharaoh's house.

Scripture gives us more examples of people who did the same, people who refused to turn to God, people who hardened their hearts and, in the process, took themselves far from God.

Saul, Israel's first king, started out well, but over time he became obsessed with his position as ruler. He focused less and less on God and His power, and more and more on his own circumstances. In the end, he was far from God, seeking counsel from a witch (see 1 Samuel 28:1–25). He had pushed himself so far away that Scripture says the LORD had turned away from him and become his enemy (see 1 Samuel 28:16).

Solomon started out in the right direction. The second child of David and Bathsheba, he was destined for greatness from an early age. The book of Proverbs stands as a legacy to his wisdom. He ruled Israel in its golden age. At the height of his power, his reputation spread throughout the known world. Yet he refused to obey the Holy Spirit. He married pagan wives—many pagan wives. Late in life, those wives led him into pagan religious practices. When he died, his heart was far from God (see 1 Kings 11:1–13).

The further you go away from God, the more difficult it is to get back. The more times you say no, the fewer opportunities you have to say yes. If God goes to the trouble of calling something to your attention, don't ignore it. It's important. That's why He's brought it up. Don't say no.

Give Him the one response that can take you down the path of repentance. Open your mouth and say, "Yes, Lord."

Regret for the past is not enough.
Remorse, alone, leads only to despair.

What do you think? There was a man who had two sons. He went to the first and said, "Son, go and work today in the vineyard."

"I will not," he answered, but later he changed his mind and went.

Then the father went to the other son and said the same thing. He answered, "I will, sir," but he did not go.

Which of the two did what his father wanted?

—JESUS OF NAZARETH, THE PARABLE OF TWO SONS, MATTHEW 21:28–31

CHAPTER 21

NO FEAR

Do not love the world or anything in the world.

—1 JOHN 2:25

Not all turning, not all change, leads to a relationship with God. There are two aspects to repentance, two essential elements: turning and believing. Having regret for the past, feeling bad about something you did or didn't do, is only half the story, only half the response God seeks. Feeling bad about what you've done isn't enough. You have to push past the emotion and get to the change in attitude and behavior. Feelings follow thought. The way you feel can be a very good warning sign about a problem with the way you're thinking.

Emotion is a tricky part of our personalities. The generation that came of age in the 1960s and 1970s grew up with the motto "If it feels good, do it." Feeling good isn't much of what Jesus meant when He said, "I have come that they may have life, and have it to the full" (John 10:10).

This current generation also views much of life through the lens of personal pleasure. Fulfillment in life, feeling good about ourselves, is a concept with which we are very familiar—doing our dream, finding ourselves. On the other hand, duty is not something we hear much about. Still, emotions can be very helpful if you use them as clues and not as the standard by which you make choices and decisions.

Of all emotions one can feel, perhaps the most crucial is fear. Not because it is a good thing, but because it is so devastatingly powerful. That's one reason Paul told Timothy not to yield to it: "For God did not give us a spirit of timidity, but a spirit of power, of love and of self-discipline" (2 Timothy 1:7).

The NIV uses the word *timidity*. The RSV uses the word *fear*. A more literal translation would be *cowardice*. Don't be a coward.

I've never played organized football, but you can't live in America without being at least conversant in the sport. We have a professional football team here in Phoenix and several colleges as well, so it's hard to miss. Professional games are on television every Sunday afternoon. College games fill almost every channel on Saturday. They even show high-school games once in a while. I'm not much of a football fan, but some things about the game are rather interesting.

Football coaches spend a lot of time training defensive linemen to react to the pressure they feel from the opposing offensive linemen. In a game, plays develop quickly. There isn't enough time for defensive linemen to think. No time to analyze or contemplate what to do. Besides not having time, people are always in the way. Big people. Even if a lineman tried to look, he wouldn't be able to see the play. The man in front of him is over six feet tall and weighs more than three hundred pounds. Seeing the quarterback behind a guy like that is next to impossible. On top of that, the guy with the ball is quick and fast. If a lineman takes the time to think about the play, the play will be past him.

So the coaches tell them to move against the pressure they feel from the opposing player. The pressure is their clue. It tells them the direction in which the play is going. If the lineman from the other team tries to push you in one direction, you work against it. You work your way in the opposite direction from the way he wants you to go. Don't think. React. React to the pressure.

Like plays in a football game, the events of life come at you fast. They come at you in ways that keep you from seeing everything all at once. I once heard someone say, "You live life going forward but only understand it looking backward." You don't always have the time you'd like to stop and comfortably analyze every situation before you make a decision. Life is moving, and you have to move with it. Stop too long, and life moves on without you, or runs you over.

That's where fear enters.

Fear is the way Satan pressures you in the direction he wants you to go. Fear is a powerful force. I'm sure you've heard of people who are so afraid of insects that if they encounter a wasp while driving a car, they are more willing to risk fatal injury by wrecking the car in an effort to get away than they are willing to be stung.

What makes someone do that?

Fear.

Fear will have you doing things you'd never do otherwise. That's why the Holy Spirit makes such a point of telling us not to let fear rule our lives.

My oldest daughter, Sevannah, has had bouts with night terrors. Some nights she wakes me up screaming at the top of her voice. The sound of it makes me bolt from my bed and race down the hall to her. When she has those episodes, I have a choice. I can help her avoid addressing the issue—I can sleep with her, I can hold her until she goes back to sleep, I can sing her a lullaby—or I can show her how to allow Jesus to help her face the fear. Holding a three-year-old in the middle of the night and telling her to invoke the name of Jesus isn't always the comfortable thing to do. It would be much easier to crawl into bed with her and lie there until she goes back to sleep. Instead, I tell her Jesus is right there with her, and He will chase away the fear. All she has to do is call on Him. We do that together. The other night I overheard her in her room doing that same thing on her own.

In the parable of the talents, who felt the wrath of the master? The one who allowed fear to dictate how he used his talent.

Then the man who had received the one talent came. "Master," he said, "I knew that you are a hard man, harvesting where you have not sown and gathering where you have not scattered seed. So I was afraid and went out and hid your talent in the ground. See, here is what belongs to you." (Matthew 25:24–25)

The response was swift and harsh: "You wicked, lazy servant!" (Matthew 25:26).

The message of that parable is obvious: Don't let fear rule your life.

Please understand me. Pressing into fear, going head-to-head with it, is not comfortable. Fear doesn't come when you're feeling strong and able. It usually comes when you're weak and vulnerable. The kids are hungry, it's late in the month, and you have five dollars in your pocket. Not five dollars with a wallet full of credit cards and money in the bank—just five dollars. Ever walk into a grocery store with four mouths to feed for dinner and five dollars to get it done? To everyone else it may look as though you're all alone, but standing right there next to you in the aisle of that grocery store is fear. Hollow, cold fear. That's when fear comes. When you're not ready. When you're vulnerable.

With fear, Satan points to your circumstances and tells you God is a liar. He tells you you're going to fail, you're stupid, God doesn't love you.

Whatever fear tells you, it's just a lie.

All those things Satan told Adam and Eve, he's telling you— all that and more. He's telling you the same things he told Jesus when he tried to tempt Him. The same thing he told Peter the night Jesus was arrested. The same thing he told Judas. You can agree with that fear and agree with the liar, or you can agree with God and press against it. God wants you to press against it. Take that fear as a witness to the validity of what you're trying to accomplish. Take it as a clue to what God is doing in your life. Take it as pressure trying to push you in a direction God doesn't want you to go. The play is developing ahead of you. Satan is trying to stop you because you are right on course for what God wants.

Work past the fear. Fear can't stop you if you keep moving. If you allow the Holy Spirit to take control, He can turn that fear into affirmation of His call on your life.

Fear is trying to drive you away from the play, away from My will.

Emotions are very powerful. That is why Satan tries to attach a lie to them. You enjoy earning money, he turns that joy into greed. You notice the beauty of your neighbor's wife, he turns it into lust. Satan watches your emotions because they come from a vulnerable aspect of your personality, an area where your defenses are weakest, and an area through which he can insert a lie. You cannot allow yourself to be content with merely an emotional response to your circumstances.

Repentance brings a change in emotion. You felt one way about something or someone, now you feel a different way. The lie Satan attaches to that emotional response is an attempt to tell you the emotional change is enough. He tells you that because he wants you to stop right there. He wants you to be satisfied with having changed the way you feel about the matter. He doesn't want you to go on to the next step, the step of a change in your conduct. Don't believe him. An emotional response alone takes you nowhere.

I'm not saying you should repress your feelings. I'm saying a change in the way you feel about something isn't enough. You have to allow God to change the way you think, the way you believe. You have to let Him change your allegiance from faith in a lie to faith in Him.

Repentance that brings conversion and repentance as a lifestyle both center on the same concepts: Turn and believe. In repentance that leads to conversion, you change your mind and change your allegiance. In a lifestyle of repentance, God changes your mind and you allow Him to change your conduct.

Feeling bad about what you've done or how you're living is a prompting from the Holy Spirit, a warning bell to get your attention, but it is only half the process. It alone will not get you any closer to God or any closer to wholeness. To get to wholeness, you have to pair that remorse, that change in how you feel, with a change in allegiance and a change in conduct. You have to accept the gift of God's presence in your life. That gift is Jesus. You unwrap that gift through acts of repentance.

Turn to Him now, and let Him work the changes in your life He knows you need. Turn to Him now while you have the opportunity. Accept the Gift.

When Judas, who had betrayed him, saw that Jesus was condemned, he was seized with remorse and returned the thirty silver coins to the chief priests and the elders. "I have sinned," he said, "for I have betrayed innocent blood."

"What is that to us?" they replied. "That's your responsibility."

So Judas threw the money into the temple and left. Then he went away and hanged himself.

—MATTHEW 27:3–5

CHAPTER 22

BEYOND REMORSE, PAST REGRET

Show us which of these two you have chosen
to take over this apostolic ministry,
which Judas left to go where he belongs.

—ACTS 1:24–25

In the parable of the two sons we saw how remorse can lead to change, or remorse can lead to nothing. That same concept appears with Judas. Scripture says that after he betrayed Jesus and saw what the authorities were going to do to Him, "he was seized with remorse" (Matthew 27:3). Judas wasn't merely feeling bad about the situation. Remorse had a hold on him. He was consumed with remorse, filled with remorse. Even though he returned the coins, his remorse led him only to a rope and the limb of a tree.

Judas has an interesting name: Judas Iscariot. Scholars have long debated what the name Iscariot means. You'd think if Scripture used the word *Iscariot* to distinguish this Judas from others with the same name, Iscariot must have an obvious meaning.

Perhaps it did at that time, but the distinction has apparently been lost. Still, the debate over what Iscariot means is interesting in the way it sheds light on how, from a human perspective, Judas never took the next step, the one from remorse to repentance. He never got past the emotion.

Judas sold out Jesus for the sake of an emotion, too: greed, and perhaps jealousy. Some have tried to soften Judas, suggesting that he betrayed Jesus under the mistaken belief that Jesus was supposed to be a political liberator of Israel, and so Judas betrayed Him to force Jesus's hand. That is not the image Scripture portrays.

According to Matthew's account, Judas decided to betray Jesus after an incident at the home of Simon the Leper. There, a woman came to Jesus with a jar of expensive perfume, which she humbly poured on His head, anointing Him. As she did so, Jesus was deeply moved, and He warmly accepted this gracious gift.

"When the disciples saw this, they were indignant. 'Why this waste?' they asked. 'This perfume could have been sold at a high price and the money given to the poor' " (Matthew 26:8–9).

Jesus calmed them down and explained to them the significance of what was happening, but in the next paragraph we see Judas's reaction.

"Then one of the Twelve—the one called Judas Iscariot— went to the chief priests and asked, 'What are you willing to give me if I hand him over to you?' So they counted out for him thirty silver coins. From then on Judas watched for an opportunity to hand him over" (Matthew 26:14–16).

There's little doubt Judas did what he did for the money. From the way the account reads, it seems obvious he was reacting to what he thought was Jesus's indifference to the supposed waste of the expensive perfume. Perhaps he thought, *If Jesus can get His, I can get mine.* Either way, he did it for the money.

Emotions are powerful, and Judas never got past his. First he was captured by greed, the love of money. Then he was trapped by feelings of remorse. Judas couldn't move beyond either of those feelings.

If Judas had pushed through the remorse he felt, he could have found forgiveness. As we discussed in an earlier chapter, Peter failed Jesus the night Jesus was arrested, standing in the courtyard when he denied ever knowing Him. All the remaining disciples ran and hid, choosing their own safety over being identified with Jesus. They all found forgiveness when they turned again to faith in Jesus. They repented of giving in to the fear and lies, and they found Jesus waiting for them with open arms.

Judas could have found forgiveness, too. But he didn't. And the reason he didn't, from a human perspective, was that he never went beyond the emotions of the moment. He never got further than the bare feeling of remorse. He did not take that emotion as a clue to guide him toward what God was trying to do in his life. Instead, he let the emotion make the decision for him. Remorse, instead of leading to life, led to death. He saw the emotion as bearing witness to the lie Satan was telling him: "Do you know what you did? Do you know who that guy was you turned in? Oh, man. You can't go back now. You blew it. Big time."

Satan always works that way. He maneuvers you into caving in to temptation. Then, when you do, he tells you you made a mistake. You blew it. You're out now.

It's all a lie.

Judas found himself in need of repentance, but repentance seemed to be out of reach. He could get as far as the emotion of remorse, but no further.

Push past your emotions. Repent now, while the opportunity is available. Repent and believe, for the kingdom of God is near.

As I prayed and sought the Lord, I saw in my mind a sea of people. They had their arms outstretched, their hands lifted high above their heads. I watched as they dropped to their knees and cried out to the Lord, begging for mercy and love to reign free in their lives and in our nation. The cry of their voices was louder than anything I'd ever heard before, a deep wailing, as if their hearts were broken. I remember my own heart breaking as I saw it.

Then I heard these words: "I have never forsaken you, nor have I abandoned you. I was there when America was hit at its core. I was there through the hurricanes, the tornadoes, the earthquakes. I was there when you lost your father and mother, your best friend, your child. I was there. It was you who turned your backs on Me, and it is time—time to bring Me back to the center. The peace, the comfort, the protection that you so desperately seek can only be found in me."

—SHAWN-MARIE COLE

CHAPTER 23

A SINGLE CANDLE

Healing rain, I'm not afraid

To be washed in heaven's rain.

—MICHAEL W. SMITH, "HEALING RAIN"

As I heard the words to this song, I began to see rain

falling across America. Then I saw the hand of God wipe

through our nation, flooding the land with its light,

bringing healing and restoration to people

and to our land.

—SHAWN-MARIE COLE

The history of our country reads like a litany of technological change.

Telegraph, phonograph, telephone.

Train, automobile, airplane.

Computer, cell phone, internet.

America is the world's entrepreneur. We have invented and reinvented ideas and technologies that have shaped life around the world. In the process, we have invented and reinvented ourselves and what it means to be an American many times over.

Change defines who we are as a people and who we are as a nation.

From the day settlers first stepped ashore on the eastern coast of this continent, America has been on the move—pressing the western boundaries of our continent and pressing the boundaries of our minds.

In the broad sweep of human history, America isn't very old. As the lives of nations go, we are one of the youngest. Yet in the brief time we've existed as a country, we've witnessed transformation and development at a rate never known in the history of humankind. Much of that change has occurred in the last fifty years.

Fifty years ago there were no personal computers, no fax machines, no ATMs. Cell phones hadn't been invented. The internet wasn't possible, and pocket calculators didn't exist. Technology is very different now than it was then.

In the first century of our nation's history, change came slowly. Information was disseminated from hand to hand. Mouth to mouth. There were no wires. No phones. No television. Except for newspapers, there was no such thing as mass communication. It took awhile for new ideas to circulate long enough to produce any results.

Now change happens quickly and we learn about it instantly. Information that once traveled at the speed of a horse now travels at the speed of light. You can sit at home and watch the president deliver an address from the Rose Garden. Stick around a few minutes longer and you can see the reaction of leaders on the other side of the world. You can watch a baseball game as it happens. Follow a policeman in New York as he chases a suspect from building to building, participate in a conference with employees thousands of miles away, track your employees as they do their jobs—all of it captured by a camera and delivered to your living room, conference room, or computer screen in less time than it takes to change the channel. As a result of instant information, the rate of change is accelerating.

We travel fast, too. We can have breakfast in London, lunch in New York, and watch the sunset that evening from a mountaintop in California. That wasn't possible fifty years ago.

Technology has changed. Society has changed, too.

Two hundred years ago, most people held a common set of beliefs about life. We had a sense of right and wrong that wasn't based on the result we were trying to achieve. Basic Christian concepts like sin, redemption, and salvation were widely understood, even if not so widely embraced.

Now that is no longer true.

When asked by polling organizations, a majority of Americans typically indicate they are Christians. Still, church attendance and church membership are in serious decline. Typical lifestyles of those claiming to be Christian are not much different from those who don't. Divorce, teen pregnancy, and abortion all occur at the same rate in and outside the church. Most people who attend church are as biblically illiterate as those who don't. Those commonly held Christian concepts of a hundred years ago aren't even understood by church members today.

Crime is on the rise. Addiction has become so prevalent we expect it—addiction to drugs, alcohol, pornography, sex, and things to which no one knew you could be addicted fifty years ago. Sex has moved from a private act to first a public fantasy and now a national obsession. Pornography is an industry. Sexual abuse is a constant threat. Sexual predators seem to lurk at every turn.

On a broader scale, terrorists threaten to destroy us. Greed destroys our corporations, taking with it the livelihood of employees who spent their careers building the company. In the process, lifetimes of retirement and investment plans, hopes and dreams, futures and families are left crushed and ruined. Hurricanes batter our coastlines, leaving a trail of devastation in their wake. Under the rubble we find a culture of corruption and waste at every level of government.

We've changed, but life hasn't gotten any better.

Not that we haven't tried. Turn on your television, and you'll see a stream of advertisements offering you gadgets to make life easier, technology to make life simpler, pills to make you stronger, smarter, sexier, younger. We've crammed so much into the void of our lives. We're awash in consumer items, luxury items, food, entertainment, sports, pets—diversions of every kind.

Do we even know what we are looking for? Could it be that the path we've taken has led us to where we are because it was the wrong path? Could it be that in all of our changing we've taken ourselves further and further from the life we want, from the life we were created to live, from the life all those changes seemed to promise?

No one can deny that our daily tasks are much more conveniently accomplished now than they were in the past. Few of us would want to go back to living with the technology available fifty years ago. We like our fax machines, personal computers, and cell phones; our double-shot lattes and our air-conditioned cars. I like them, too.

What threatens us is not the changes in technology but the changes in American culture. And, yes, those changes really are a threat.

You remember earlier in this book we talked about the consequences of lifestyles lived beyond the boundaries set by Scripture—the methamphetamine addict with rotten teeth and abscesses on his skin, the destruction of families brought on by infidelity, the unwanted pregnancy occasioned by sex outside marriage. Those consequences come from a much deeper dilemma. That dilemma is the cheapening of human life.

I'm not talking about the policy position of your favorite politician on some hot-button political issue. I'm talking about how cheaply *we* view life—not how cheaply the government views it, but how cheaply you and I view it.

We don't care about the poor. We don't care about the hungry. We don't care about the way materialism has consumed us. We don't care about whether we actually live the lifestyle Jesus modeled for us. All we care about is ourselves. That's a cheap view of life. That's a view of life inconsistent with Scripture. That's a wrongly held belief, and it provides a place for Satan to get a toehold in our lives. Left unaddressed, that toehold becomes a stronghold, a fortress of death and destruction in our lives.

Just as our personal repentance permeates our relationships, bringing life and transformation to our families and friends, so also the consequences of our individual choices reverberate across our entire nation.

You can't avoid it. No one lives to himself or herself. Our culture arrived at the place it is today because individuals made choices that took us in that direction. We've moved far from the life God wants for us. But know this: It's we who have moved. Not God.

The call to repent and believe, to accept the gift of repentance and receive the gift of God's transforming presence in our lives, is a call that carries with it the key to changing the direction of our nation. It is a call that has recurred through the ages and one we dare not ignore.

That offer of the gift of repentance, and through it the gift of mercy and grace, is the same offer God made through Jonah to the ancient city of Nineveh: "The word of the LORD came to Jonah son of Amittai: 'Go to the great city of Nineveh and preach against it, because its wickedness has come up before me' " (Jonah 1:1–2).

The wickedness of Nineveh was not the wickedness of a collective entity but the wickedness of individuals—a city of individuals. God's message to them was clear: "Forty more days and Nineveh will be overturned" (Jonah 3:4).

Forty days. That message sounds like a proclamation of pending doom, but that is just the point. Pending. Judgment had not yet been executed, and the fact that it was announced forty days in advance meant there was still time. Time to repent. And that is what they did.

"The Ninevites believed God. They declared a fast, and all of them, from the greatest to the least, put on sackcloth" (Jonah 3:5).

They believed God. They turned from what they had been

doing and believed. They repented—turned and believed, turned and changed.

When the king heard about it, he repented, too.

Do not let any man or beast, herd or flock, taste anything; do not let them eat or drink. But let man and beast be covered with sackcloth. Let everyone call urgently on God. Let them give up their evil ways and their violence. Who knows? God may yet relent and with compassion turn from his fierce anger so that we will not perish. (Jonah 3:7–9)

Give up their evil ways. Give up their violence. Turn to God. Turn and believe. Repent and change. The Ninevites of that day gave us a perfect picture of repentance and a perfect picture of how individual repentance can change the course of history for a country.

The call to repent is an individual call. A call to an individual act. I am called to repent of my sins, not yours. Likewise you are not called to repent of my sins or those of anyone else. We each stand on our own before God. But that is not the end of the story.

Remember, no one lives only to himself or herself. What I do affects my neighbor. What my neighbor does affects me. Together, the circumstances of our lives are intertwined in the effects of the lifestyles we choose. A lifestyle of repentance, of allowing Him to reign, brings one result. Rebellion brings quite another. The effects of those choices flow to us and to our neighbors. Those choices affect the ebb and flow of the worldview of an era. The cultural wave that swept through the 1950s brought sweeping changes in music. That wave moved on to the late 1960s and early 1970s, influencing drug use and sexual liberation, but that wave was one of individual choices. There was no collective decision, no collective choice applicable to the whole. Those changes came from individuals making lifestyle choices about who would rule in their lives.

Choices to put ourselves in charge can be reversed. We have the option of choosing to exercise the gift of repentance. That choice will transform our lives, and it will transform our nation. Let God Reign Down in your life, and He will Reign Down in our nation.

National repentance sounds like an obvious extension of the general notion of personal repentance—
certainly governments have engaged in atrocious
conduct. Personal repentance leading to acts of national repentance is a tempting leap to make. But
this raises the question of repenting of a historic act,
an act of a past generation and, more to the point,
raises the question, can I repent of my neighbor's
sin?

CHAPTER 24

THE MYTH OF NATIONAL REPENTANCE

The first and fatal charm of national repentance is,
therefore, the encouragement it gives us to turn
from the bitter task of repenting our own sins
to the congenial one of bewailing—but, first, of
denouncing—the conduct of others.

—C. S. LEWIS, *THE GRAND MIRACLE*

In the preceding chapters we have traveled across the land-scape of repentance from repentance that leads to conversion, to a lifestyle of repentance, to a change of emotion that may or may not lead one to God. Finally now we have come to explore how God can transform a nation through individual repentance. Throughout our discussion we have talked about repentance as a personal act as opposed to a corporate act. We have discussed it that way because that is the way Scripture discusses it.

Today we often hear people call for collective, corporate acts of national repentance. This is at first glance an inviting proposition. Over the history of our republic, our government has enacted many policies and engaged in many actions, both here and abroad, that have brought pain and grief to individuals and entire races of peoples. That we should now repent of those policies and actions has a certain ring of logic to it, a certain appeal to the mind and intellect.

I live in Arizona, part of the Great American West. Of all the things for which America is famous, the West must be the most distinctive—cowboys, cattle drives, gunfights, and Indians.

Ah, yes, the Indians.

If ever there were a list of national policies for which someone should repent, the way we treated Native Americans would be at the top of the list.

Every year tourists make the trek out to Arizona to visit the Grand Canyon. It's a wonderful, majestic example of the beauty God has built in to His creation. I've been there myself. There is nothing quite so awesome and inspiring as looking down from the rim of the canyon at a place far below—a place you think is the canyon floor—only to see a silvery sliver in the distance and realize that this thin ribbon is the Colorado River winding its way across the true canyon floor, much farther below and away in the distance.

If you go out to the eastern end of the canyon, you enter a Navajo reservation.

Reservation. It sounds so benevolent. We reserved a part of this state just for you.

Drive through that reservation some day after you've seen the grandeur of the canyon. Not much is out there in that wide expanse. Just gently rolling hills, tall buttes, and scraggly sagebrush. Perhaps the Navajo like it that way, nothing and no one for miles and miles. I hope they do. They weren't given much choice about the matter, or the location.

Imagine having the entire region all to yourself, to roam and live and raise your family, and then one day a group of strangers shows up and takes it from you. In the process of taking the land, they slaughter your relatives, rape your friends, herd you from place to place like animals. Then, as a gesture of goodwill and a nod to human dignity, they give you first one area, then change it for another. Then, finally, they give you what's left over, the part the strangers think is useless.

If we were honest, that's how we would view that reservation: land for which we have no obvious use. I'm sure the people who live there see the beauty of it, but the only reason anyone allowed them to have it was because no one saw any use for it. If there were a use for it, if there were oil under it, or water, or minerals, we'd find a loophole in the treaty that established the reservation, and we'd take *that* land from them, too.

That's what we did in the past. But they aren't the only people we treated that way.

People in the Old South have witnessed all too often the effects of abhorrent national policy. Slavery was a practice that should never have been allowed anywhere, and certainly not among people so noble as to suppose that everyone is "endowed by their Creator with certain unalienable rights."

Yet slavery was the official policy of our government, both state and federal, from the time Europeans first set foot on this continent. And it was a policy that proved very difficult to eradicate. We're still struggling with vestiges of it.

We had to fight a war to get rid of slavery and then fight a hundred years more to outlaw segregation. Now we're fighting to alleviate the economic and educational inequities engrained in our society by four hundred years of an awful governmental policy.

Very tempting to suggest we should have an act of national repentance. Very tempting to think there is something we can do collectively to erase the wounds.

But I am not called to repent of my neighbor's sin. I am called to repent of my own.

Throwing everything off as a "national sin" might be salve to my conscience, but it does nothing to bring healing to my soul. For that, I must examine my own soul.

Think about the national issues for which we are often urged to repent. Some suggest we repent of the sin of abortion. Others the sin of racism. The way we treat people in the Middle East. The way we treat developing countries.

While I would agree that those things are wrong, the question I should ask is not, Why did "they" do that or believe that or hold those opinions. The question I should ask, the question I must ask is, Do I?

"National repentance" lets me lay all my sin on someone or something else, some collective "we" that lets me off the hook and leaves me feeling as though I've really done something. That is a dangerous thing to do and a dangerous place to be.

Someone once said, and I don't know who it was or I would attribute the quote to the person, "If Satan can't get you to do something wrong, he'll deceive you into doing something good." That's what happens when we succumb to the notion of "national repentance."

Repentance, personal repentance, is that thing, that action, that practice to which God calls us. Repentance that leads to conversion, repentance that delves deep into who we really are. Searching, revealing repentance that gets to the core of our habits, our attitudes, our beliefs. That is our calling. It is a calling to a lifestyle of personal repentance—repent and believe; repent and change.

A supposed call to national repentance is a diversion, a cheap substitute, a lie. National repentance sounds good, but it keeps us from the real question. It keeps *me* from the real question, the question about me.

If you want to change our nation, and surely you must, that change must start with you.

Take, for example, one of the most divisive issues: abortion. It is very easy to point a finger at the judges, the doctors, the politicians, and the advocates and accuse them of murdering millions of babies. That is an easy thing to do, and many have done it. But what about our own personal attitudes toward sex? Oh, yes, we say we're against premarital sex. We say sexual activity should be reserved for the sanctity of marriage. But in practice that is not what we do. There is little difference between the sexual practices among those who claim to be Christian and those who profess no religion. Depending on which poll you read, some 80 percent of Americans claim to be Christian. If that is really true, why is the rate of teen pregnancy so high?

We say we're in favor of "family values." We value the family as a unit and hold to a lofty biblical view of it. Yet we accept repeated divorce and remarriage, in effect sanctioning serial polygamy, in contradiction to Jesus's own teaching on the subject, a teaching the disciples found so restrictive that they said, "If this is the situation between a husband and wife, it is better not to marry" (Matthew 19:10).

How can the world hear our message if our actions don't match the words coming from our mouths?

We say we must love all and treat everyone the way Jesus would. WHAT WOULD JESUS DO? is a slogan you can find on wristbands for sale in almost any store in the country. Yet we exempt certain groups of people from that slogan. Gays and lesbians and abortionists are groups that quickly come to mind as people for whom we reserve a different rhetoric—the "we hate you, and you're lost" rhetoric.

Would someone struggling with his or her sexual identity come to you for guidance? Would a woman with serious questions about how to handle a pregnancy come to you for advice?

We are not called to count off the sins of our neighbor, but that is what "national repentance" urges us to do. That isn't a call to biblical repentance, but a call to point out the sins of everyone else. And that is heresy.

We are called to worship God and to lead others to worship Him as well. The path to worship begins with repentance. Repent and believe, in response to His call to worship Him, to join Him in a journey of repentance, going deeper into you and deeper into Him.

National repentance, if there is such a thing, comes only as we each repent, one by one, for the things God shows us in our own lives.

To silence those voices, you need to repent, honestly, and ask God to forgive you. That judge inside your heart, our conscience that judges you, will stop judging you only when you come to terms with God. And those videos will stop playing in your mind only when you truly repent and God forgives you.

—JOHN RUCYAHANA,
THE BISHOP OF RWANDA

CHAPTER 25

A VISION OF NATIONWIDE REPENTANCE

You have to be truthful so that you can pass on truth
to your children. If you lie, you will pass on
those lies to your children, and your children will
pass them on to your grandchildren.

—JOHN RUCYAHANA, *THE BISHOP OF RWANDA*

As I said in the previous two chapters, national repentance is a lie. However, nationwide repentance is a good thing. A vision of nationwide repentance compelled us to write this book. That vision of nationwide repentance—a nation of people all repenting as individuals—is the key to our personal wholeness and a key to our national future.

We Christians say we believe God is the God of the universe. We say, as God spoke through Daniel long ago, "The Most High is sovereign over the kingdoms of men and gives them to anyone he wishes" (Daniel 4:25).

We know what God has said about His expectations for those kingdoms of men: "He has showed you, O man, what is good. And what does the LORD require of you? To act justly and to love mercy and to walk humbly with your God" (Micah 6:8). We know the standard. We can see we have not met it. Nationwide repentance—millions of us humbling ourselves, saying yes to Him, handing over control of our lives, yielding ourselves to a probing, searching journey of repentance that takes us to a place of personal wholeness and completion—is the way to fulfill His expectations for us. He doesn't want some collective act of repentance. He wants a collection of people who have individually repented. A nation of people who actively follow a lifestyle of repent and believe, repent and change, repent and worship.

The power of that sort of act, of a nation of individuals who have and are repenting, is an amazing thing to behold.

Perhaps no place on earth better demonstrates the power of nationwide repentance, as opposed to the erroneous notion of national repentance, than the country of Rwanda.

In 1994, nearly one million Rwandans were killed, murdered, slaughtered, hacked to death in one of the worst periods of ethnic cleansing ever to occur on earth. The Hutus, backed by the Rwandan government, carried out a carefully orchestrated plan, long in the making, to wipe out the Tutsi people. They very nearly succeeded. Between victim and perpetrator, practically every family in the country incurred the direct effects of a wave of terror unimaginable to the human mind. Men, women, children—all cut down in the most gruesome manner.

Still, the people of Rwanda have found a path to reconciliation. That path is the path of confession, repentance, forgiveness, and restitution. Not through corporate services of some vague and mollifying work of "national repentance" but through the real, gritty, intensely personal work of ministering to both the victims and the offenders, bringing them face-to-face in an exercise of personal reconciliation. One of the keys to that process is the personal act of repentance—not repentance for some idea of sin or for some general notion of sin, but for the real, inhuman acts that nearly obliterated an entire people.

Slowly, change is coming to the country of Rwanda, not because of government-imposed policy, though the current government has helped immeasurably, but because of the personal acts of repentance carried out by individuals. Much of the work has been accomplished through prison ministry and prisoner programs led by the church of Rwanda and assisted by Prison Fellowship International and Saddleback Church of Lake Forest, California.

During that year of terror, and even after the major atrocities ended, horrible things were done. Unspeakable things. Things that ought never to have occurred. Moving the country away from those events is not something that can be accomplished by mere public gatherings in which people lay their own sins off on some impersonal, collective "country," or "nation," or "we."

Reconciliation, change deep enough to affect the course of a nation, can only come from deeply personal, searching repentance. A lifestyle of allowing the Holy Spirit to search the depths of your sense of self, the depths of your soul, the depths of who you really are, and allowing Him to make you the person He really wants you to be. The people of Rwanda are taking that journey, and it is moving their entire country to a place of wholeness and blessing.

In the United States, we face racism on a far more subtle level. Do you quickly grow impatient with a person who doesn't speak fluent English, maybe even thinking, *He should just go back to where he came from if he can't speak the language?* Do you lock your car doors when you're stopped at an intersection and see a couple of teenage boys of a different race crossing the street near you? Do you think of people of different races or cultures as "lazy," "dirty," "ignorant"?

We need to allow the Holy Spirit to reach these deeply held attitudes, the ones that come up in derogatory remarks (or thoughts) while we wait in a slow-moving line, or when we're passed over for a job or miss a scholarship that is given to a member of another race. Those attitudes come from the same place in us that produced more heinous acts experienced by those in Rwanda. Personal repentance of those attitudes is the only thing that will get us to the wholeness and completion God offers us.

And racial issues aren't the end of our troubles.

The world has a long history of abusing women. Misogyny, the hatred of women, is still passed from generation to generation. Watch a few minutes of some TV shows that feature footage of police officers making actual arrests. You'll see what goes on in homes across the country. In more polite circles, that same hatred is often conveyed subtly, through cutting and bruising remarks rather than outright physical beatings.

Pornography, prostitution, and an assortment of sexual conduct for hire have become so pervasive in our society it is now referred to collectively as the "sex industry." Go online and do a search on the subject. You'll find page after page of search results leading to articles about trafficking in women for use in the sex trade, about men who travel to Asia to have sexual relations with minor children of both genders. It will make you sick—so sick you'll want to repent of reading the articles, but you cannot close your eyes to the victims' pain and hopelessness.

No, you don't have to repent of the conduct of others, but you have to allow the Holy Spirit to examine your own conduct. You say the prurient sexual practices of others are horrible, you say the sex industry should be shut down. Do you visit pornographic sites on the internet? Do you read books and magazines that glorify and promote those degrading acts?

We're often called upon by well-intentioned spokespeople to repent of our profligate lifestyles that have us sloshing around in food while much of the world starves. Well we should repent, but not nationally. Not for my neighbor's obsession with food. I should repent of my own obsession with it. You should repent of yours. We eat more in one meal than much of the world has all day—more than some have for an entire week. Look around you. Look in the mirror. Many of us are well above a healthy weight. Yet we regard the hungry with callous indifference, and we regard our own attitude with that same indifference: "I can't do anything about their situation. I'm not in Sudan. I'm in Ohio. It's lunchtime. Let's go eat."

Repentance begins with you. Not the nation. Not your neighbor. Not someone you think is in worse shape than you. Repentance begins with you.

Transformation awaits us. God awaits us, and offers us the fruits of His work in our lives, but first we must yield to Him.

What He said to Solomon long ago He says to us today: "If my people, who are called by my name, will humble themselves and pray and seek my face and turn from their wicked ways, then will I hear from heaven and will forgive their sin and will heal their land" (2 Chronicles 7:14).

God was not talking about a collective turning, separate and apart from a personal turning. Not a turning as in some act of "national repentance" that makes us feel good for the moment, but rather a turning to Him in individual acts of repentance that take us deeper into ourselves and deeper into Him.

The nation will not change until we change. And we will not change until we turn to God and give Him the only response we have to give, the response from which all repentance begins. The response that exercises the gift of repentance and accepts the Gift. That response is simple.

"Yes, Lord."

"Yes, Lord. Be the Lord of my life."

"Yes, Lord. Reign and rule over me."

"Yes, Lord."

Say yes to Him. He will reign over you and rain down His mercy and grace. Let Him Reign Down.

AN EXERCISE IN PERSONAL REPENTANCE

Now the Lord God had planted a garden in the east . . .

—GENESIS 2:8

All the way through this book we've been talking about the need to do something, to act, to say yes to God. If you skipped to this appendix to see how the book ends, don't stop reading. Finish it, and then go back and read the rest of the book to catch up.

The point of this book is to bring you to a place of repentance in your life, to introduce you to a lifestyle of repentance. We want to help you do that. We want you to repent—not just read about it and not just think about it.

To help you, we'd like to take you through an exercise, an exercise of repentance. If you're into training and physical fitness, think of this as repentance weight training.

Here's what we want you to do. (It'll work better if you read all the way through this chapter and then do the exercise.)

Get yourself in a place where you won't be interrupted for a few minutes, a room where you can close the door. Or go outside to the backyard and sit in a lawn chair. Stretch out on a blanket on the beach. Lock yourself in the bathroom. Any place where you won't be interrupted for a short while.

Once you're in a private place, get yourself in a comfortable position. Sitting would be better than standing. Lying down might be too comfortable, but if you're already stretched out on the beach, don't get up. You need to be comfortable, but don't go to sleep.

After you're in a comfortable position, take a deep breath. Then let it out.

Close your eyes and feel your body relaxing from your scalp down to your neck, down to your hips, all the way down your arms to your fingers and down your legs to your toes. Feel your muscles relax as you let the tension ease from them. Allow that sense of relaxation to ooze down from your head to your neck, your hips, your legs, your feet, all the way down to the soles of your feet.

Now, imagine you are in a garden. A beautiful garden. You are walking down a path in that garden. It's a pleasant, sunny day. Around you are lovely flowers and shrubs. Jesus is walking along with you. You and He are admiring the flowers.

That garden is your life.

As you walk along, you come to a weed. That weed is growing right there with the flowers. See that weed in your mind. It may be a large weed. It may be small. Just let your mind see it.

Now see yourself bending over to pull it up.

You grasp it with your hands and pull. The ground around it is moist and soft. It comes up by the root. Completely by the root. You are holding that weed in your hand, and you turn to Jesus.

That weed represents the thing of which you need to repent.

Ask Jesus the name of that weed—not a botanical name, but the name of the thing in your life the weed represents. He will tell you. Wait for Him.

When He tells you the name, remember it. Then hand Him the weed.

See the weed disappear in His hand.

Now articulate to Jesus in a prayer what just happened.

Thank Him for showing you whatever it was you needed to repent of, and say these words: "Lord Jesus, I repent of _____." Fill in the blank with whatever He showed you. Ask Him to send His Holy Spirit to assist you in following that thing all the way out to the end of its roots in your life, just as you saw in that garden. Ask Him to make that repentance real in your life and to seal His work by sending the Holy Spirit to that area of your life from which that weed came.

Some of you may find it hard to see the value of an exercise like this, but it will help you visualize the act of repentance. It helps to take away some of those old images we have of repentance. Seeing repentance as a walk in the garden with Jesus is much better than seeing it as a glowering, angry preacher pointing his finger in our faces and reminding us how bad we've been.

You can repeat that garden exercise as often as you need it. Perhaps you could make it a part of your daily time with God, at least for a season. Try it. He's waiting to take a walk with you in the cool of the evening.[1]

NEW TESTAMENT CONCEPTS OF REPENTANCE

The New Testament uses three words to discuss repentance. Before your eyes glaze over and your mind checks out, let me say this. I don't care much for word studies. They sound nice from the pulpit, and the speaker gets to show how much he or she knows about Greek or Hebrew, but word studies usually start off tedious and end up dry. Sermons with that approach to Scripture come across very much like a classroom lecture, which most of us slept through, and I think that's what most congregations do, too.

Getting to the bottom of a word, tracing a linguistic path back to its origin, takes us back through thousands of years of written and spoken language, much of it buried in obscurity. Doing that makes it very easy to add more meaning into a word, and into a verse, than was ever intended by the writer—or the Holy Spirit.

The kind of Hebrew used to write the Old Testament and the kind of Greek used to write the New Testament are both versions of languages that are no longer spoken. Ancient Hebrew wasn't even used at the time of Jesus, at least not as a daily language. In typical conversation, Jesus spoke Aramaic, something akin to Hebrew slang. Ancient Hebrew had already passed out of use by the time He was born, as had classical Greek.

When it comes to particular words, the minute details aren't usually the point anyway. Most of the power of Scripture comes through the obvious. Jesus had a sense of humor, and He might have been coy at times, but He came to reveal Himself, not to hide the truth. Most of the time, His point was easily found. So, I'm not big on word studies.

Having said that, and having indulged myself in showing off how much *I* know about Hebrew and Greek, understanding a few things about how Scripture conveys the concept of repentance might be helpful as you implement the principles in this book.

The New Testament uses three words to describe the notion of repentance: *epistrepho*[1] (epy-stref-o), *metanoia*[2] (meta-noy-a), and *metamelomai*[3] (meta-mell-o-my).

The first word, *epistrepho,* is usually translated as the English word *turn,* though in the book of Acts it is the word for "conversion." The second word, *metanoia,* usually is translated as "repent." The last, *metamelomai,* is sometimes rendered as "repent," but a more literal rendition would be "regret." These three words are different enough in meaning that the writer's choice in using one or the other cannot be merely stylistic. That means we can't lump them all together as meaning exactly the same thing. We have to think about each one separately for a moment.

Epistrepho is the word used to describe what we would call conversion, a complete and total reorientation of a person from one worldview to another. Like many Greek words, *epistrepho* conveys two ideas wrapped up together, giving you both ideas all at once. Those ideas are turning and believing. "I tell you the truth, unless you change and become like little children, you will never enter the kingdom of heaven" (Matthew 18:3). The word *change* in the NIV makes the sentence read easily in English, but it glosses over the enormity of the meaning conveyed by Jesus's statement. A literal rendering of the Greek word would be "unless you turn," as in "turn into a child." If you want to enter the kingdom of heaven, you have to turn into a child, a physically impossible assignment for an adult. That impossibility gives you a sense of the magnitude of the change Jesus was talking about here. You must become something that is impossible for you, in and of yourself, to become.

This is the same word used in Acts to describe what happened to the Gentiles who heard and responded to Paul's preaching: "The church sent them on their way, and as they traveled through Phoenicia and Samaria, they told how the Gentiles had been converted" (Acts 15:3). Converted, from nonbelievers to believers. From pagan infidels to citizens of the kingdom of God. To be clear, from enemies to friends. A total transformation of allegiance. They were living lives totally devoted to the enemy, and then they turned to follow Jesus—a turning in the opposite direction with the emphasis on the new direction, not the past.

With this word, *epistrepho,* the emphasis isn't on the thing from which you've turned, but on the one to whom you've turned. It doesn't focus on the bad things you used to do or the way you used to believe or the lord you used to serve. Instead, it focuses on the change of lordship. You have sworn fealty to a new king: the King of kings.

The second word, *metanoia,* includes the idea of turning, but it emphasizes the thing from which you've turned, not so much the one to whom you've turned. This word looks back toward the past, toward some worldview or past conduct or former belief from which you are now turning. You're still turning, definitely and decisively turning, but this word is used to point your attention toward the thing from which you turned. For example, "In those days John the Baptist came, preaching in the Desert of Judea and saying, 'Repent, for the kingdom of heaven is near' " (Matthew 3:1–2).

Because this word points to the act of turning and to the thing from which you've turned (but not to the one to whom you're turning), Scripture often reinforces and expands the meaning and implication of that act by coupling the word *metanoia* with the word for "believe" in the familiar phrase "repent and believe," as in Mark 1:14–15: "After John was put in prison, Jesus went into Galilee, proclaiming the good news of God. 'The time has come,' he said. 'The kingdom of God is near. Repent and believe the good news!' "

Turn from the old life. I have good news for you. The New Life is here. Reject your former ways. The kingdom of God is at hand. Good news.

The third word, *metamelomai,* occurs only a few times in the

New Testament. This word describes the emotion associated with some act or belief, the feeling of remorse. It does not denote any sort of turning away from anything except a turning from a prior emotion. You felt one way about something or someone, then your emotions changed and you felt another way. It is used in the New Testament to convey only the emotion of regret. Jesus used this word when He told the parable about the two sons, one who agreed to help his father but never showed up and the other who refused to help but later changed his mind (sometimes translated "repented") and came back.

"There was a man who had two sons. He went to the first and said, 'Son, go and work today in the vineyard.'

" 'I will not,' he answered, but later he changed his mind and went" (Matthew 21:28–29).

He changed his mind. He was irritated about being asked to work, then later felt bad about telling his father no. In this instance, the change of mind led to a change of action, but that change of action or conduct is not implicit in the word alone. *Metamelomai* conveys only a change in emotion.

This same word is used to describe the remorse Judas felt over what he'd done in betraying Jesus to the Sanhedrin. When he first went to the Jewish authorities and conspired with them to hand over Jesus, he felt one emotion; perhaps he felt he was doing something good. Then, after he saw what happened to Jesus and what He was about to endure, Judas felt bad. He felt remorse. Perhaps he felt an agonizing, cold sense of despair, as if standing before an abyss with an arctic wind in his face, but there was no change in his relationship with Jesus. His sense of remorse took him no further than that emotion.

"When Judas, who had betrayed him, saw that Jesus was condemned, he was seized with remorse and returned the thirty silver coins to the chief priests and the elders. 'I have sinned,' he said 'for I have betrayed innocent blood' " (Matthew 27:3–4).

We all know what happened after that.

These three words taken together can give us a broad view of the biblical idea of repentance. Repentance begins with conversion, *epistrepho,* surrendering your life to Christ, a reorientation from self to God. That turning is complete the moment you make the decision to make Jesus Lord of your life. You have moved to a new kingdom, and you aren't going back to the old one. The turn is complete, but you are not.

For the completion of Christ's becoming real in your life, you have to go with Him on a journey into yourself and into Him. On that journey you will find yourself continually turning from unbelief to belief in a cycle of repent and change, repenting of beliefs that in the beginning you were not even aware you held, beliefs that form the root of many of the habits and attitudes that have plagued you your entire life. Here the emphasis isn't on turning as in conversion, but on turning from particular things, the notion conveyed by our second word: *metanoia.*

Then, there is bare regret: *metamelomai.* The feelings of remorse, despair, and regret. This word conveys only a sense of change in emotion. You felt one way about something, then something happened, and you felt differently. A change of emotion that may, or may not, lead one to faith in Christ.[4]

BIBLIOGRAPHY

Bakker, Jim. *I Was Wrong.* Nashville: Nelson, 1996.

Bodishbaugh, Signa. *The Journey to Wholeness in Christ.* Grand Rapids: Chosen, 1997.

Brown, Colin, ed. *The New International Dictionary of New Testament Theology.* 4 vols. Grand Rapids: Zondervan, 1975.

Cash, Johnny. *Cash: The Autobiography.* San Francisco: HarperSanFrancisco, 1997.

Clairmont, Patsy. *I Grew Up Little.* Nashville: W Publishing Group, 2004.

Colson, Charles W. *Born Again.* Mechanicsburg, Pa.: Crossings Classics, 1976.

Cruz, Nicky. *Run Baby Run.* Orlando, Fla.: Bridge-Logos, 1988.

Curry, Dayna, and Heather Mercer. *Prisoners of Hope.* Colorado Springs: Waterbrook, 2002.

Eldredge, John, and Stasi Eldredge. *Captivating.* Nashville: Nelson, 2005.

Graham, Billy. *Just As I Am.* San Francisco: HarperSanFrancisco, 1997.

Graham, Franklin. *Rebel with a Cause.* Nashville: Nelson, 1995.

Heche, Nancy. *The Truth Comes Out.* Ventura, Calif.: Regal, 2006.

Holmes, Michael W., ed. *The Apostolic Fathers.* Translated by J. B. Lightfoot and J. R. Harmer. Grand Rapids: Baker, 1989.

Lewis, C. S. *The Grand Miracle.* Edited by Walter Hooper. New York: Random House, 1970.

———. *Mere Christianity.* New York: Simon & Schuster, 1952.

———. *The Problem of Pain.* New York: Simon & Schuster, 1962.

Moore, Beth. *Get Out of That Pit.* Nashville: Integrity, 2007.

Omartian, Stormie. *Stormie.* Eugene, Ore.: Harvest House, 1986.

Rucyahana, John. *The Bishop of Rwanda.* Nashville: Nelson, 2007.

Schaeffer, Francis A. *Genesis in Space and Time.* Downers Grove, Ill.: InterVarsity, 1972.

Waddell, Helen. *The Desert Fathers.* New York: Vintage Books, 1998.

Walsh, Sheila. *The Heartache No One Sees.* Nashville: Nelson, 2004.

Waltrip, Darrell, and Jay Carty. *Darrell Waltrip: One-on-One.* Ventura, Calif.: Regal, 2004.

Wilkerson, David. *The Cross and the Switchblade.* Grand Rapids: Revell, 1993.

Visit our website at www.ReignDownUSA.com.

NOTES

Chapter 2: The Key

1. While *metanoia* is the most commonly used word, the New Testament actually uses three different words to describe repentance. See Appendix 2 ("New Testament Concepts of Repentance") for a discussion of all three.

Appendix 1: An Exercise in Personal Repentance

1. See also Signa Bodishbaugh, *The Journey to Wholeness in Christ* (Grand Rapids: Chosen, 1997).

Appendix 2: New Testament Concepts of Repentance

1. Greek επιστρέφω
2. Greek μετάνοια
3. Greek μεταμέλομαι
4. For a more complete discussion of topics addressed in this appendix see "Conversion, Penitence, Repentance, Proselyte" in *The New International Dictionary of New Testament Theology,* ed. Colin Brown (Grand Rapids: Zondervan, 1975), 2:353ff.

DISCUSSION QUESTIONS

Chapter 1: Reign Down

1. When someone is transparent about some event or failure in life, what is the common human response to such openness?

_____

_____

_____

_____

_____

2. How long is your list of personal failures or emotional traumas that you need to share with someone you trust?

_____

_____

_____

_____

_____

DISCUSSION QUESTIONS

Chapter 2: The Key

1. Why doesn't the listing of good behavior produce the desired life change?

_____

_____

_____

_____

_____

2. Jesus was often criticized by religious leaders for spending time with "unclean" people. Do any religious people ever level that same charge at you? If not, why not?

_____

_____

_____

_____

_____

Chapter 3: Just Say Yes

1. If the gospel is not about how good you are, what is the focus of the message?

_____

_____

_____

_____

_____

2. What is the first step in repentance?

_____

_____

_____

_____

_____

Chapter 4: Stop Hiding

1. What are some of the methods you observe that people use in order to try to hide from God?

_____

_____

_____

_____

_____

2. When you are personally trying to hide from God, what are some of the reasons for that avoidance?

_____

_____

_____

_____

_____

DISCUSSION QUESTIONS

Chapter 5: In an Instant

1. What does it mean to suggest that repentance begins in an instant?

_____

_____

_____

_____

_____

2. How can one person repent for another person?

_____

_____

_____

_____

_____

Chapter 6:
An Instant, Long Time Coming

1. Why do you think our society tries to limit the definition of what sin is?

_____

_____

_____

_____

_____

2. How would you define the word *sin*?

_____

_____

_____

_____

_____

Chapter 7: But Wait! There's More!

1. From literature to personal observation, we all see that the trappings of the "good life" do not bring happiness, yet people still desperately strive for those trappings. Why do you think this is true?

_____

_____

_____

_____

_____

2. What about the "good life" is the most enticing to you?

_____

_____

_____

_____

_____

Chapter 8: Detours and U-Turns

1. Deep down, do you often feel that Christians deserve to have things turn out good in their lives?

   _____

   _____

   _____

   _____

   _____

2. What are some specific areas that repentance might demand a relinquishing of control?

   _____

   _____

   _____

   _____

   _____

Chapter 9: Turning Point

1. Sometimes God uses major life events to catch our attention. Have you missed the message in your own life?

   _____

   _____

   _____

   _____

   _____

2. Is there someone in your life you can be honest with about your own heart? Is your heart cold? Is it closed? What will it take for you to open up?

_____

_____

_____

_____

_____

Chapter 10: Contagious Repentance

1. In listing the five people you are closest to, are they people who have a spirit of repentance? If not, why not?

_____

_____

_____

_____

_____

2. Would your closest friends affirm that you have a heart of repentance? How do they see that in your life?

_____

_____

_____

_____

_____

DISCUSSION QUESTIONS

Chapter 11: A Lifestyle

1. During the reading of this book, what is something you have learned about the gift of repentance?

   _____

   _____

   _____

   _____

   _____

2. As you honestly examine your life, what area of your lifestyle most needs to be turned over to God again and again?

   _____

   _____

   _____

   _____

   _____

Chapter 12: Starting with the Big Stuff

1. Do you have a tendency to minimize your own personal sins and magnify the sins of others? In what areas are you the most critical? The most accepting?

   _____

   _____

   _____

   _____

   _____

2. If you were able to remove two sins from your life, what would they be? What are you doing to remove them?

_____

_____

_____

_____

_____

Chapter 13: It's All Big Stuff

1. Where (physical place) is your alone place with God?

_____

_____

_____

_____

_____

2. The last time you were alone at that place with God, how did he work in your heart?

_____

_____

_____

_____

_____

Chapter 14: Even the Preacher

1. How is it that people find themselves being so busy doing good for God that those good things result in distance from God?

_____

_____

_____

_____

_____

2. How can you keep from doing things simply for the performance?

_____

_____

_____

_____

_____

Chapter 15: Dangerous Vows

1. Have you bought into a lie that has limited your submission to God? If not, are you suggesting you are the only person who has not?

_____

_____

_____

_____

_____

2. Are you comfortable talking about your past, or are you fearful of what you might discover?

_____

_____

_____

_____

_____

Chapter 16: No Condemnation

1. Jesus isn't interested in beating up on his people, so why do you think we do it so much?

_____

_____

_____

_____

_____

2. If Jesus does not condemn his people, why do many live with so much self-condemnation? How can people move beyond that evaluation?

_____

_____

_____

_____

_____

DISCUSSION QUESTIONS

Chapter 17: True Freedom

1. What steps does your local Christian community (church) take so as not to become modern-day Pharisees?

   _____

   _____

   _____

   _____

   _____

2. Do you have such a strong attitude against a specific group of people that your attitude might hinder them from seeing the love of God? Which group of people do you verbalize against the most?

   _____

   _____

   _____

   _____

   _____

Chapter 18: Letting Go of the Wheel

1. What specific area of your life needs the greatest surrender to God?

   _____

   _____

   _____

   _____

   _____

2. Would your closest friends describe you as a control freak? Even more important, what areas of your life does God know you still battle to control?

_____

_____

_____

_____

_____

Chapter 19: Transformation

1. What are the two biggest mistakes you have made in your life?

_____

_____

_____

_____

_____

2. Do you really believe that God can make something incredible out of the mistakes of the past? Or do you secretly think you are the exception to what God promises?

_____

_____

_____

_____

_____

Chapter 20: RSVP Required

1. Are there areas of God's invitation you continue to say no to?

_____

_____

_____

_____

_____

2. Do you delight in spending time with God? And if not, have you ever thought about why that might be true?

_____

_____

_____

_____

_____

Chapter 21: No Fear

1. What is the greatest debilitating fear you have?

_____

_____

_____

_____

_____

2. Who do you fear disappointing the most, yourself or God?

_____

_____

_____

_____

_____

Chapter 22:
Beyond Remorse, Past Regret

1. What emotional baggage most contributes to your hesitancy to turn things over to God?

_____

_____

_____

_____

_____

2. How can you turn emotional insecurity into an effort to trust the promises of God?

_____

_____

_____

_____

_____

DISCUSSION QUESTIONS

Chapter 23: A Single Candle

1. While all the technological changes have made the speed of information transfer almost instantaneous, what part of your heart changes the slowest?

   _____

   _____

   _____

   _____

   _____

2. Since people change one heart at a time, what are you doing to assist others in changing?

   _____

   _____

   _____

   _____

   _____

Chapter 24:
The Myth of National Repentance

1. If "national repentance" keeps us from the real question, what is that real question?

   _____

   _____

   _____

   _____

   _____

2. What are some of the areas of injustice our nation still needs to address?

_____

_____

_____

_____

_____

Chapter 25:

A Vision of Nationwide Repentance

1. How did the people of Rwanda move toward reconciliation as a country?

_____

_____

_____

_____

_____

2. Since you have not slaughtered thousands, how does the incredible story of Rwanda penetrate your own heart?

_____

_____

_____

_____

_____